An Integrated Approach to Character Education

An Integrated Approach to Character Education

Editor
Timothy Rusnak

CORWIN PRESS, INC.
A Sage Publications Company
Thousand Oaks, California

For information:

Corwin Press, Inc.
A Sage Publications Company
2455 Teller Road
Thousand Oaks, California 91320
E-mail: order@corwin.sagepub.com

SAGE Publications Ltd.
6 Bonhill Street
London EC2A 4PU
United Kingdom

SAGE Publications India Pvt. Ltd.
M-32 Market
Greater Kailash I
New Delhi 110 048 India

Printed in the United States of America

Library of Congress Cataloging-in-Publication Data

Main entry under title:

An integrated approach to character education / edited by Timothy
Rusnak.
    p. cm.
  Includes bibliographical references and index.
  ISBN 0-7619-0437-9 (cloth: acid-free paper) —
  ISBN 0-7619-0438-7 (pbk.: acid-free paper)
  1. Moral education—United States. 2. Character—Study and
teaching—United States. 3. Curriculum planning—United States.
4. Active learning—United States. 5. Classroom environment—
United States. 6. Community and school—United States. 7. School
management and organization—United States. I. Rusnak, Timothy.
LC311.I68 1997
370.11′4—dc21   97-21186

This book is printed on acid-free paper.

98 99 00 01 02 03 10 9 8 7 6 5 4 3 2 1

Production Editor: Astrid Virding
Editorial Assistant: Kristen L. Gibson
Production Assistant: Denise Santoyo
Copy Editor: Stephanie Hoppe
Typesetter/Designer: Janelle LeMaster
Cover Designer: Marcia M. Rosenburg
Indexer: Teri Greenberg

Contents

Principle One

Character Education Is Not a Subject; It Is Part of Every Subject

Principle Two

Integrated Character Education
Is Action Education

Principle Three

A Positive School Environment
Helps Build Character

Principle Four

Character Development Is Encouraged
Through Administrative Policy and Practice

Principle Five

Empowered Teachers Promote Character Development

Principle Six

The School and Community Are Vital Partners in Developing Character

Preface

An *Integrated Approach to Character Education* describes how almost 20 years of systematic cross-cultural research on the issue of character acquisition has evolved into successful classroom and school practices. It is a resource designed for K-12 school administrators, curriculum specialists, and those concerned with the inclusion of character education in schools. It is a useful text for teacher educators and other university faculty who have a research or teaching interest in the area of educational foundations, instructional techniques, learning environments, or related courses that explore the emergence of educational theory in actual classroom practice. It may be particularly useful as a resource or general text for educators interested in educational administration, as the contents focus on the development and implementation of curricula, school leadership, and classroom organization.

There are two distinctive features of this text. First is the hopeful view of the integrated approach to character education. Building on a carefully developed international study of character development that forms a theoretical platform, teachers and scholars worked in concert to identify six principles of integrated character education that foster academic success and help children to become productive and contributing members of society.

The second distinctive feature of the text is a rare glimpse of how the thinking and theory that emerge from the laboratory of the university manifests in the practices of schools and classrooms. This is an evolutionary process that few educators have an opportunity to witness.

Although the six principles form the blueprint for the integrated approach to character development, it must be stressed that no one principle is designed to be better or more important than any other principle. Additionally, as will be seen, schools have found success in dealing with only one principle rather than assuming the formidable task of addressing all the principles together.

This approach proposes an effective and action-oriented way of addressing the sensitive issues of values and character growth in our schools. The chapter authors remind us that what we currently describe as character development has always been a part of successful schooling. Occasionally overlooked and often misunderstood in our schools, character education is ever powerful in its ability to shape the academic and social growth of our youth.

ORGANIZATION

The text contains six basic sections. Each section represents a principle of the integrated approach to character education. Each section is then divided into two chapters. The first chapter of each section is authored by a university scholar who discusses the research that forms the foundation for the principle. The second chapter of each section is authored by a public school teacher or administrator who describes, through his or her own experiences, the implementation of the principle in actual schools. The text is followed by an epilogue and summary of many current character education programs so that educators and parents may begin to make decisions about specific programs that may best suit their schools.

In the introduction, Timothy Rusnak examines the elements that set the integrated approach apart from other character education programs and outlines the six principles that form the integrated approach to character education.

Timothy Rusnak introduces the first principle of integrated character education in Chapter 1. In connection with this principle—*Character education is not a subject; it is part of every subject*—he discusses why character growth has been and continues to be so important in our schools and communities. Rusnak presents the rationale for including character in curriculum and daily lessons and links successful teaching to character building. William Switala, in Chapter 2, highlights how the integration of character in the curriculum and daily lessons of the school have played such a powerful role in positively shaping the academic and social lives of the students in his district.

In Chapter 3, Thomas Farrelly introduces us to the second principle of integrated character education—*Integrated character education is action education.* Farrelly examines the emerging dimensions of the developing child and describes how an action-oriented character education program leads to a morally mature individual. James Antis describes his regionally recognized work in action-oriented teaching in Chapter 4. Antis outlines some instructional tactics that he and teachers in his school use to promote character growth through action. He reminds us that character education recognizes the importance of solid classroom instruction but also advocates the necessity of involving our youth in activities to strengthen their commitment to themselves and others.

Mark Tierno addresses the third principle of the integrated approach to character education in Chapter 5—*A positive school environment helps build character.* Tierno clarifies the complex web of interactions that form the life of the growing child and shows how teacher modeling promotes a positive classroom environment that may help children grow socially and academically. Kenneth Barbour, in Chapter 6, draws on his three decades of experience in inner-city schools to describe ways in which teachers have made a difference in the lives of children by building classroom and school environments that are positive and that promote the building of character.

Chapter 7 examines the fourth principle of integrated character education—*Character development is encouraged through administrative policy and practice.* Using his original research, James Henderson demonstrates how "authenticity" fosters an administrative leadership style that promotes character growth in a classroom, school, or district. Robert Myers, in Chapter 8, gives us a firsthand look at an administrator who promotes leadership in his district by focusing on ethical policies and practices. Myers reflects on his years of experience as a school administrator and discusses specific examples of how an ethical leadership style has enhanced his school district by promoting character development through administrative policy and practices.

Frank Ribich, in Chapter 9, addresses the fifth principle of integrated character education—*Empowered teachers promote character development.* Ribich discusses the critical role teachers play in the development of a productive learning environment by focusing on a constructivist approach that empowers teachers and children. In the tenth chapter, Judy Heasley outlines some of her work with challenged learners. She profiles some teaching approaches that successfully empower teachers and promote character.

Robert Agostino introduces us to the sixth principle of integrated character education in Chapter 11—*The school and community are vital partners in developing character.* Using a historical approach, Agostino examines early American community values and how many of these values influenced the work of John Dewey, whose educational theory has helped shape our ideas about schooling today. In Chapter 12, Donna Milanovich reflects on her years of experience as a classroom teacher and administrator in developing strong community and parental ties with schools. This chapter demonstrates how the inclusion of parents and community agencies in schools is a powerful force in character development.

In the epilogue, Paul Black draws on his many years of experience as a classroom teacher and a teacher educator to examine the important role teacher educators play in developing teachers who foster character growth in our youth. Black outlines a number of successful programs that will help teachers, administrators, and parents in starting a character education program.

ORIGINS OF INTEGRATED CHARACTER EDUCATION

Integrated character education traces its roots to a comprehensive international research project that began in 1980. A group of leading scholars, representing universities from throughout the world, met in Spain to discuss the importance of culture and values in society. These academics formed the Council for Research in Values and Philosophy, with the intent to respond to the need for research related to the development of responsible persons through education.

The council initiated a research project entitled Foundations of Moral Education. For the work in the United States, it was decided to form three 10-person teams of philosophers, psychologists, and educators to address the problem from the perspective of their own discipline and to engage in discussions with those from the other disciplines. Over the next several years, this careful study began to shape a view of moral education for our schools that provided a sound academic base and was appropriate for a pluralistic society such as the United States.

By the mid-1980s, the first phase of the project was completed with the publication of three scholarly works that act as the foundation for the project. In *Philosophical Foundations of Moral Education and Character Development*, edited by George F. McLean, Frederick E. Ellrod, David Schindler, and Jesse A. Mann (1991), scholars analyzed various theories of moral development and discussed classical and phenomenological philosophical approaches to understanding the person. Special attention was paid to the educational implications for moral growth. In the text *Psychological Foundations of Moral Education and Character Development: An Integrated Theory of Moral Development*, edited by Richard T. Knowles and George F. McLean (1992), academics addressed the psychology of moral emotions and moral choice, storytelling, and character development. A theoretical structure was refined for understanding moral growth, with an analysis for the potentialities and approaches to moral education at each age level from early childhood to old age. *Character Development in Schools and Beyond*, edited by Kevin Ryan, Thomas Lickona, and George F. McLean (1992), explores the nature of moral education and character development and focuses on the school as an essential environment for promoting moral growth. The work examines the classroom and curriculum at the various levels and addresses education's relation to family, religion, media, and community. Teams of scholars were formed in Latin America, Asia, and Africa to expand the approach developed in these three volumes and to articulate the values of their own particular cultural traditions as the basis for their own moral education programs. To date, 24 volumes of international scholarship constitute the research foundation of this ongoing project.

In 1985, Duquesne University's School of Education was asked to join the research project. Less than a year later, the Center for Character Education, Civic Responsibility, and Teaching was formed to act as an implementation agent in this emerging view of character development. The primary purpose of the center was to distill the massive theory into classroom practice. The center was designed to enhance the theoretical elements of the project by using actual classroom tactics designed by teacher educators, classroom teachers, and administrators in a cooperative effort that truly wed theory with the realities of schools.

By summer 1987, the Duquesne Center began conducting workshops for educators. These workshops created the unique opportunity for classroom teachers, school administrators, and parents to work hand in hand with the international scholars who formed the original project and to assist in crafting a meaningful program for schools, thereby merging theory with classroom practice.

From the outset of the workshops, it became apparent that several central elements of the research project distinguished this view of character development from others. First was the systematic scope of the ongoing scholarship. Generated in Europe, developed in the United States, and extended internationally, it is research of an unparalleled dimension as it examines the acquisition of values in cultures from around the world. The work analyzes contemporary character education programs and suggests a new view of the acquisition of character.

In the integrated view of character education, cognition is a part of moral development, not a means to an end. The impact of social environment, culture, and emotion also plays an important part in the development of an individual's character. Moreover, the integrated view of character developments relies on action rather than only moral reasoning through discussion to enhance character growth.

For 3 years, in summer workshops, monthly colloquia, and weekly seminars, teachers representing a cross section of school and grade levels worked with the scholars who founded the theoretical base of the project. Gradually, a usable blueprint for promoting character growth in schools emerged in the form of six basic principles, which are also described as the integrated approach to character education. These educators concluded that the teaching of character is less about "making bad kids good" than about recognizing that character formation is the very nature of teaching.

REFERENCES

Knowles, R. T., & McLean, G. F. (Eds.). (1992). *Psychological foundations of moral education and character development: An integrated theory of moral development* (2nd ed.). Washington, DC: Council for Research and Values and Philosophy in Education.

McLean, G. F., Ellrod, F. E., Schindler, D., & Mann, J. A. (Eds.). (1991). *Philosophical foundations of moral education and character development*. Washington, DC: Council for Research and Values and Philosophy in Education.

Ryan, K., Lickona, T., & McLean, G. F. (Eds.). (1992). *Character development in schools and beyond*. New York: Praeger.

About the Contributors

V. Robert Agostino is Program Director for Secondary Education in Duquesne University's School of Education. He also coordinates the innovative doctoral program in instruction, which emphasizes instructional leadership and excellence. A full professor, he teachers social studies methods classes and historical foundations courses. A Boston College graduate, he started as a junior high school teacher and continued his professional training at the University of Bridgeport, Connecticut. His concerns for teaching excellence led him to Ball State University, Muncie, Indiana, where he completed his EdD in social science education. His interest in character education was marked by his sponsorship in the 1970s of the first values education workshop held at Duquesne and by his ongoing emphasis in his teaching on character development, values, and moral training.

James Antis is Principal of Horace Mann Elementary School in the Indiana School District in Indiana, Pennsylvania. Prior to becoming an elementary school principal, he served in a number of positions, including assistant senior high school principal and acting principal at both elementary and secondary levels. Before his administrative experiences, he was an art teacher in the junior and senior high schools in the

Plum Borough Schools in suburban Pittsburgh. He earned his bachelor's degree in education at Edinboro University of Pennsylvania and his elementary and secondary administrative certification as well as his doctorate in education from Duquesne University. He is also a graduate of the Air Force Officers School of Military Science.

Kenneth Barbour is Elementary School Principal in the Riverview School District near Pittsburgh, Pennsylvania. Prior to his current position, he served for 30 years in the Pittsburgh public schools as a classroom teacher and school principal. He is also the former superintendent of the Wilkinsburg School District. He received his doctorate in educational administration from the University of Pittsburgh and has consulted in many schools in the area of curriculum design and character development.

Paul F. Black is Professor and Chair of the Secondary Education/Foundations of Education Department, University of Pennsylvania at Slippery Rock. Prior to this position, he was a secondary classroom teacher and taught at the University of Akron, the University of Pittsburgh, and the Pennsylvania State University, where he specialized in the area of education policy and instructional methodology. He earned his doctorate at the University of Pittsburgh, and a master's in education at Duquesne University. He currently serves on three national committees of the Association of Teacher Educators, was elected to the board of directors of the state affiliate, and has presented numerous papers to regional and national organizations in the area of teacher education and restructuring. He also serves on the advisory board of the Center for Character Education, Civic Responsibility, and Teaching and was a Scholar in Residence there in 1995.

Thomas Farrelly is Emeritus Professor and former Director of the Center for Character Education, Civic Responsibility, and Teaching at Duquesne University. After studying at the National University of Ireland and Fribourg University in Switzerland, he received a doctoral degree in education from the University of South Florida. His primary focus is on curriculum development for character education. He has done research on moral education in U.S. schools and worked for 4 years as a consultant with the Kenya Ministry of Education and Nairobi University on the development of a national curriculum for moral education. He has written widely in the field of moral education and was editor of a series of textbooks on the issue published by Oxford University Press and used in Kenyan high schools.

Judy Heasley is Supervisor of Special Education programs for the Midwestern Intermediate Unit IV and serves as Principal of the Clarence Brown Education Center in Butler, Pennsylvania. She has also worked as the behavior management consultant, the early intervention case manager, and a special education teacher for that intermediate unit. She has taught numerous continuing education courses and provided extensive staff in-service training workshops and seminars. She has also served in a number of capacities for the local, regional, and state Pennsylvania State Educational Association. She is a graduate of Clarion State University, where she also earned a master's degree in special education, and is currently pursuing postgraduate studies at Kent State University in Ohio.

James E. Henderson is Professor and Dean of the School of Education at Duquesne University, where he also directs the Interdisciplinary Doctoral Program for Educational Leaders (IDPEL). Prior to his most recent post, he served as the superintendent of schools in the Montgomery (New Jersey) Township Schools; as superintendent of schools and assistant superintendent for personnel in the Reading (Pennsylvania) School District; as assistant superintendent for business, high school principal, and vice principal in the Upper Freehold (New Jersey) Regional Schools; and as a middle school unit leader and high school teacher in the East Windsor (New Jersey) Regional Schools. He has won a number of awards for his leadership in schools and community agencies and has authored numerous articles in journals and professional publications. Most recently, he has attracted national attention for his work in win/win collaborative negotiations, in school-based decision making, and in leadership selection and development.

Donna K. Milanovich is Principal of J. E. Harrison Middle School in the Baldwin-Whitehall School District, Pittsburgh, Pennsylvania. A graduate of Duquesne University, she began her career as an elementary teacher and a secondary guidance counselor. She earned a doctorate in administrative and policy studies at the University of Pittsburgh. A strong advocate for young adolescents, she is a member of the Pennsylvania Middle School Association (PMSA) Executive Board, currently serving as the organization's president. She is a director of the Middle

Level Academy—a PMSA/Duquesne University initiative established to promote middle-level teaching practices. A recognized leader in middle-level education, she is the recipient of the Ann Moniot Outstanding Middle Level Educator of the Year and the Kirk Distinguished Service Awards.

Robert D. Myers is former Superintendent of Schools of the Fox Chapel Area School District in Pennsylvania. During his 37-year career in education, he has served as a classroom teacher, guidance counselor, principal, and superintendent. He received his doctorate degree from Nova Southeastern University.

Frank M. Ribich is Professor of Education and Chair of the Department of Educational Services in the School of Education at Duquesne University. He directs the student teaching program and coordinates the field experience program. He served basic education as a teacher of English, social studies, and Spanish and as a guidance counselor, supervisor of foreign languages, and administrator. He earned degrees from Duquesne University and the Pennsylvania State University and studied at the University of Pittsburgh as a postdoctoral student. His contributions to higher education are in program design at the undergraduate and graduate levels, portfolio development and assessment, and phenomenological validation procedures.

Timothy Rusnak is Director of the Center for Character Education, Civic Responsibility, and Teaching at Duquesne University in Pittsburgh, Pennsylvania. Prior to joining the faculty at Duquesne, he worked in basic education for nearly 20 years as an elementary and middle school teacher, social studies curriculum coordinator, and instructional team leader in the elementary and middle school grades. He received his doctorate in education from the University of Pittsburgh in 1980 and has participated in a number of extended learning experiences, including at Harvard University, where he studied at the Moral Education Institute under the direction of Lawrence Kohlberg. He is very active in a number of professional organizations, including the Association of Teacher Educators (ATE), where he holds a seat on the Character Education Commission. He is the past president of the Western Pennsylvania Council for the Social Studies, has consulted in many schools, and has presented and authored numerous papers dealing with the issue of character development and learning environments.

William J. Switala is Visiting Assistant Professor of Education at Duquesne University in Pittsburgh, Pennsylvania, where he teaches classes in social studies methods and curriculum. Prior to teaching at Duquesne, he was a classroom teacher for 15 years and an administrator for 16 years in public education. As Curriculum Director for the Bethel Park School District, near Pittsburgh, Pennsylvania, he chaired the district Character Education Committee and helped to implement several character education initiatives. He received his BA degree from St. Vincent's College with a major in philosophy and his MA degree in classics from Duquesne University. He also holds a PhD in classics from the University of Pittsburgh.

Mark John Tierno is Campus Executive Officer and Dean at the Sheboygan Campus of the University of Wisconsin. He held a number of administrative and teaching positions in higher education over the past 30 years. During his career in education, he has been a middle school teacher, curriculum designer, and instructional team leader in basic education. He has worked in dozens of schools with hundreds of teachers searching for better ways to effect learning. He received his doctor of arts degree from Carnegie Mellon University and serves as a Distinguished Associate in the Center for Character Education, Civic Responsibility, and Teaching at Duquesne University.

Dedication

This book is dedicated to Dr. Kenneth Burrett, Professor of Education at Duquesne University. Ken was to have contributed to the
development of this text, but his sudden and untimely passing on February 14, 1997, leaves a void in us all.

To Ken Burrett, teaching was a value-laden activity. He believed
that schools were strengthened when teachers were mindful of the profound power that values play in the shaping of our lives. Therefore,
Ken advocated that we could improve teaching, and hence the quality
of our schools and society, by examining and expanding on how teachers use values in their lessons and throughout the school day.

Ken was a visionary, blessed with wit and wisdom. When many
educators hesitated to address the issue of values and character growth,
Ken Burrett broke with the conventional thinking of the time and co-
founded the Center for Character Education, Civic Responsibility, and
Teaching at Duquesne University in the mid-1980s. He tirelessly
worked to improve teacher education at all levels by aiding in the
building of innovative undergraduate and advanced degree programs
for teachers and administrators. His energy was boundless and he
seemed to be everywhere for everyone. He will be missed by us all.

Introduction:
The Six Principles of
Integrated Character Education

TIMOTHY RUSNAK

Current character education programs are largely built on fear. They respond to the litany of problems besetting U.S. society and chronicled daily in newspapers, television, radio, and magazines. Sex, drugs, and violence are only a few issues cited as reasons to inoculate our youth with a healthy dose of character education. The basic line of defense in the battle to restore order to society and rescue civilization as we know it lies in building character in our youth, or so the thinking goes.

This often well-intentioned line of reasoning is apt to lead to little more than a temporary solution. Kits, banners, flags, posters, and all the other "trinkets" of superficial programs will most certainly find their way to a storeroom by the next semester. They will be quickly forgotten along with the pricy workshop that accompanied them. These "pop-ed" approaches only add to our rapidly expanding collection of educational fads that do not serve real needs and result in further criticism of our schools. There are more substantive reasons to teach character education in our schools than the "plug the leaky dike" approach.

THE NATURE OF TEACHING

A more productive way of looking at character education is by recognizing the nature of our role as teachers. Teaching is driven by goals, and values are an intrinsic part of goals. When a teacher selects materials, develops curriculum, asks questions, teaches a lesson, sets standards, or manages a classroom, to name only a few routine duties, the teacher is modeling a specific set of values, such as responsibility, cooperation, trust, respect, and caring. Teachers are always influencing the character of each student. Try as we might, teaching cannot be extracted from the building of character. It is the nature of teaching.

Therefore, teachers are moral agents and do more than merely pass on knowledge. The relationship between the teacher as a moral agent and the person being taught involves sharing a general values structure. Knowledge is only a tool; to activate knowledge a person needs values that act as catalysts that help form decisions and ultimately action. We witness this interactive drama played out daily in our schools. The great science teacher has students do more than memorize facts; the class gets involved in experiments that excite students and inspire their passion for learning. The exemplary math teacher does not only require students to memorize a formula; the class solves problems and goes beyond the cognitive elements of the subject. The success of the literature-based movement in our elementary schools demonstrates that reading is much more than a set of skills to be mastered.

Yet, in recent times the teacher's role as a moral agent has been dreadfully confused in well-intentioned efforts to omit a values dimension in the classroom and reduce the function of the teacher to only that of an information giver. This can be seen in a constellation of school programs that place an extraordinary value on a seemingly endless cycle of tests designed to measure the academic pulse of each student.

Sometimes it is best to look back in order to look ahead. Although often criticized, our schools have enjoyed times of preeminent status and have been the envy of societies around the world. A spate of historical evidence points to character education as a primary tool in the building of good and successful schools. It was found in Horace

Mann's triumph in the founding of the U.S. public school. Character education was very much a part of the great secondary school movement of the late 19th century. John Dewey's progressive ideals and the reforms of the post-World War I era continuously used character education as a fundamental platform for reform. Even through the "Perfect Citizen" era of the 1950s, when conformity overrode individuality in society, we find that the building of character was an important tool and rationale for school programs. These were decades when the public pridefully supported schools and enjoyed the benefits of character education. Throughout these periods, character education labored under a number of different names and has been taught in different ways, but through careful examination we find that character education was at the nucleus of school success and reform.

Even today, schools that stress character are envied for their academic excellence and social achievements. Values teaching is an important part of the life of our most successful public schools, and just witness the private sector and religious schools. Armed with an unapologetic set of values, these schools consistently produce some of the most academically talented students in the world, and they do it without police patrolling the halls and metal detectors in doorways. Again, we consistently find that these outstanding schools, both public and private, recognize that knowledge alone does not breed success and that teachers are more than conveyers of information. To such successful schools, character education is a natural part of teaching.

For West Hills Academy in the city of Pittsburgh schools, an experimental values approach helped stem a growing tide of violence and disrespect in the school. For Allen School in Dayton, Ohio, a values approach propelled a small school to unprecedented heights in academic achievement. Character education is the bond that unites knowledge, values, and action. At a time when we are looking for serious reform in our schools, the integrated approach to character development may give us a viable framework for success.

SIX WAYS TO STRENGTHEN OUR SCHOOLS

Integrated character education: These three words may reshape how we look at our schools. The term *integrated* is used to emphasize the importance of three vital characteristics of teaching and learning: *thinking—*

what is to be done or learned, *feeling*—appreciating what is learned, and *action*—experiencing through deed and not only discussion what is being learned. The word *character* is used to fix our attention on helping children discern right from wrong. Finally, *education* suggests that character may be taught. Taken together, integrated character education proposes six basic principles that foster strong academic growth while focusing on the social skills necessary to help build contributing members of society. These principles are

1. *Character Education Is Not a Subject; It Is Part of Every Subject*

Character education is part of the academic and social life of every student. It is not a course or subject; it is every subject. Teachers tend to focus on a curriculum that outlines skills and content knowledge, but always buried in the content are lessons of responsibility, respect, cooperation, hope, and determination—the essence of good character.

2. *Integrated Character Education Is Action Education*

Integrated character education goes beyond discussion and simulation. The morally mature person, as defined by the Association for Supervision and Curriculum Development (1988), "Reflects Human Dignity. . . . Cares about the welfare of others. . . . Integrates individual interests and social responsibilities. . . . Demonstrates integrity. . . . Reflects moral choices. . . . Seeks peaceful resolution of conflict." Education for the morally mature person involves commitment and action.

3. *A Positive School Environment Helps Build Character*

Teachers who are conscious of their roles as models and leaders of our young are successful because of the positive conditions they create in their classrooms. Students profit from role models functioning in an environment that encourages self-actualization and reflection. The integrated character education approach asserts that schools must be proactive and supportive of students.

4. *Character Development Is Encouraged Through Administrative Policy and Practice*

Administrators have significant influence in determining the environment in schools. Just as teachers model their behavior to enhance character growth in students, administrators must model policy and practice that demonstrate and reflect the mature character of schools and communities. As curriculum and board documents provide the benchmarks for evaluating districts, so administrators must reflect the goals of character development.

5. *Empowered Teachers Promote Character Development*

Integrated character education maintains that the teacher influences instruction far beyond the management of curricula. As the teacher is the decision maker who works in harmony with parents and community to demonstrate and influence the development of character, it is imperative that the teacher function with autonomy and wisdom. To do so requires knowledge and understanding in values and character development and a well-developed sense of self.

6. *The School and Community Are Vital Partners in Developing Character*

In the United States today, children are very often raised by single parents or no parents at all. It has been estimated that over a quarter of our children live in poverty. Success in developing character in our youth, once jealously guarded by the family, now resides in the strength of our schools and communities.

Integrated character education is not today's education gimmick. It is a product of years of research, but tempered with a practical and commonsense approach to teaching by educators. The approach recognizes the fundamental importance of academic rigor in our schools, yet it is mindful of the power of values.

The integrated approach to character education is increasingly being embraced by educators and the public, because it offers tangible solutions and great hope for our schools and society. As will be seen in the following pages, to develop character in our children is the very nature of teaching. Integrating character education in the life of the school can secure productive lives for our children and enhance the quality of our schools and communities.

REFERENCE

Association for Supervision and Curriculum Development. (1988). *Moral growth in our schools.* Bloomington, IN: Author.

Principle One

Character Education
Is Not a Subject;
It Is Part of Every Subject

1

Integrating Character in the Life of the School

TIMOTHY RUSNAK

Director, Center for Character Education,
Civic Responsibility, and Teaching
Duquesne University

"To educate a man in mind and not in morals is to educate a menace to society."

—Theodore Roosevelt (1904)

Across the country, a growing number of people are realizing the importance of teaching character in our schools. We are recognizing that even as our schools must afford children every opportunity to learn how to read, write, and compute, the real challenge to U.S. education lies in how our classrooms may foster a greater sense of personal and civic responsibility among our youth. This is character education.

Yet, there is uncertainty about the place of character education in schools. Concerns largely focus on the question, how can character be taught without creating an environment of biased values? Critics lament that the discussion of character issues is like a "hot tub" approach to education, with students sitting in groups and reflecting on their beliefs. These critics often ask, why spend valuable academic classroom time on this issue when there is no evidence that teaching character does much of anything?

What follows is a response to these central questions about character education. Through discussion of these positions, we may best understand how to integrate character education in our schools.

HOW MIGHT CHARACTER BE TAUGHT?

Character education has long been a part of our schools. Under a number of titles, ideas of teaching children right from wrong, of accepting personal responsibility, and of contributing to the community have been an important force in shaping U.S. society. Much of the strength of our political, economic, and social system may be traced to some type of approach that taught character to our children in schools.

Curriculum development and teaching are character-building activities. Both educational theorists and curriculum designers point out that curriculum planning in itself is a value-laden activity, as it gives meaning to the curriculum (Beauchamp, 1975; Goodlad & Richter, 1966; Keen, 1975; Noddings, 1995; Taba, 1971; Taylor & Richards, 1985; Tyler, 1975). The decisions on what to include in a curriculum involve value judgments. For example, the selection of textbooks, materials, stories, framing of questions, and development of concepts and skills all involve the act of valuing. A teacher who attempts to neutralize the curriculum by excluding character elements such as responsibility, honesty, cooperation, and hope sends the message that these profound concepts are not important enough to discuss.

Other professions are beginning to realize the importance of developing values and promoting character through curriculum and lessons. The C. Everett Koop Institute, for example, developed a curriculum for medical students that stressed spending more time with patients and families than in lecture halls, the intent being to develop a physician who not only knows medicine but is also responsive to the emotional aspects of the medical profession. The Albert Einstein College of Medicine is another example: Students "helped design their human values curriculum so that they could learn how to respond to their psychological needs at various stages of life and to understand their own feelings" (McNeil, 1996, p. 47).

Research has highlighted five basic elements that teachers and curriculum planners should consider when writing curriculum or teaching specific lessons (Wynne & Ryan, 1993). The elements include

1. How to focus students' attention on the ethical dimension of the story
2. How to lead students to thoughtfully consider ethical principles
3. How to focus students' attention on the moral aspects of a historical event and how to analyze and discuss it
4. How to engage students in the moral of a story and get them to see how it may apply to their lives
5. How to build among students the skills of moral discourse, which is not just casual argumentation but serious thinking about what is correct and about the "oughtness of life"

In addition, however, the essential element of *action* must be built into lessons and curricula. For example, while studying a unit on the environment in science class, teachers would normally lead discussions and lessons on the practice of our responsibility to the environment. But teachers can energize these lessons and discussions by requiring students to take action by cleaning a park, planting a tree, or maintaining a watershed area and thereby provide meaning to learning. In this way, ethical ideas come alive though central values such as prudence, justice, temperance, fortitude, faith, hope, charity, and duty (Wynne & Ryan, 1993).

Tom Lickona (1991) illustrates the power of a curriculum that focuses on character development in describing a school project in Portland, Maine. Six values—respect, courage, honesty, justice, willingness to work, and self-discipline—were systematically infused in the public school curriculum. Additionally, a leadership committee suggested curricular and lesson guidelines to all teachers in specific subject areas. For example, guidelines to instill and teach the value of self-discipline included

- Science and math teachers can focus attention on the lives of prominent men and women.

- English teachers can draw models of self-discipline from the study of literature.
- History teachers can direct attention to specific moments in history when great men and women exhibited self-discipline.
- Art and music instructors can examine the lives of great artists and composers as models of self-discipline.
- Home economics and industrial arts teachers can stress the role of self-discipline.
- Physical education and health teachers can show students that one must maintain a certain degree of self-control to maintain a healthy body. (Lickona, 1991, pp. 166-167)

The promotion of character has been widely and successfully used in the building of curricula. Whether it be described as an affective dimension, gaining attitudes and appreciations, or used as an organizing principle, the movement toward developing character in the curricula is a powerful force in our schools. It helps shape the school environment, teaching tactics, and school administration. Character education enhances responsibility, respect, cooperation, and hope—the very concepts needed to promote academic growth. More important, it helps shape the lives of students to become better contributors to the social, political, and economic fabric of our society.

DOES CHARACTER EDUCATION WORK?

George Madus, a nationally respected researcher and test author, notes, "When you have a high stakes test, the tests eventually become the curriculum. It happened with the Regents exams in New York" (quoted in McClellan, 1989, p. 644). The high stakes Madus refers to are the very issues that concern political and business leaders when they chide our schools for failing to produce academically talented people who can compete in a global and highly competitive economy. The net result has been to shift curricula away from the promotion of character and toward a more academically focused, test-oriented approach.

Paralleling this obsession about academic testing has been an inability to measure, with any scientific accuracy, the development of character. The movement toward the affective domain, or the acquisition of attitudes of learning, as proposed by Krathwahl, Bloom, and Masia (1967) and, more recently, Knowles (1992) in describing the concept of affectivity and a moral imagination, is largely held in question by a great many researchers who focus on measuring specific outcomes through factual tests.

The business axiom, "If you can't measure it, you can't manage it," has lessened the focus on teaching character in U.S. schools in recent years. Character education has largely been replaced by the belief that schools should singularly focus on academic growth. This approach has met little success, as test scores overall remain unacceptability low and many children lag behind some Third World nations in testing achievement.

But great teachers foster character growth in their classrooms. In 1995, the *New York Times* correspondent Kimberly J. McLarin interviewed 20 award-winning teachers from across the country. Each of these outstanding teachers expressed strong support for the teaching of values and while reflecting on his or her own teaching style consistently spoke of teaching character.

McLarin set out to find out what these honored teachers meant when they spoke of teaching values and character. She followed one award-winning teaching back to her school in New Jersey and carefully observed the teacher for one full school day. The reporter concluded that everything the teacher did, from daily academic lessons to routine hall and lunchroom duties, in some way addressed the issue of character building. It was this process of building character by addressing values that distinguished this teacher from others in the building.

Ron Bowes knows what life is like in the classroom. Bowes was a classroom teacher in the city of Pittsburgh schools for over 20 years and developed successful programs in some of the most difficult schools in the city. Currently, he is the assistant superintendent for public policy for the 126 Pittsburgh Catholic schools. In analyzing the differences between public and private education, Bowes observed,

> What makes the difference? Teaching values makes the difference, a values orientation, that is why we don't have a fraction of the discipline problems that are found in the public systems, and 9 of every 10 of our students go on to college and are successful— and keep in mind that we're not talking about a handful of students, we are the fourth largest school system in the State of Pennsylvania. (personal interview, August 6, 1996)

Project PAVE is yet another example of the positive power of character education in our schools. In 1990-1991, the Wisconsin state legislature implemented a government-funded tuition voucher plan in the Milwaukee public schools. This plan permitted up to 750 students to attend nonreligious private schools in Milwaukee. In 1992, a group of business and religious leaders raised enough money to expand the voucher program for low-income families to include religious schools that emphasized values and character growth. This was described as Project PAVE (Partners Advancing Values in Education), and it served roughly 2,370 students enrolled in 102 different private schools during the 1993-1994 academic year.

In analyzing the PAVE program, Beales and Wahl (1995) reported these key findings:

- PAVE students outperformed all other students on standardized academic tests.

- The PAVE program cut across social, racial, and economic groups. For example, 57% of the PAVE families are headed by a single parent. About one half of the students are white; over one third are African American; one sixth are Hispanic.

- Ninety-six percent of PAVE parents are satisfied with the quality of their child's education.

- Although the majority of PAVE students attend Catholic schools, the program also includes Muslim, Jewish, and non-Catholic Christian schools.

The PAVE program clearly demonstrates that schools that emphasize character growth also positively influence student academic achievement. Students are successful and parents are again excited and supportive of their schools. As the report concluded: "PAVE students who had come from private schools performed significantly better on standardized tests, suggesting that school environment (i.e., public or private) directly influences student performance" (p. 1).

Project Essential in Kansas City, Missouri, is another example of how the power of character education can transform schools. Focusing on concepts such as self-esteem, moral reasoning, character, and integrity, the project systematically trains teachers in curriculum development, teaching practices, and classroom organization. After a multiyear

pilot program and evaluation study, researchers concluded, "Students who receive the program are observed to display true forms of self-esteem-empathy for others, self-discipline, a recognition of their own responsibilities, and respect for the rights of others" (Project Essential Group, 1995, p. 44).

In St. Louis, Missouri, Project PREP (Personal Responsibility Education Process, 1995) was founded by business and school leaders when they realized that positive character traits were crucial in developing successful adults. School districts from the region joined to comprehensively address values such as honesty, respect, responsibility, humanity, cooperation, self-esteem, perseverance, goal setting, and service. Working with parents, community organizations, and businesses, Project PREP was at the center of a school transformation that significantly reduced behavior problems and improved academics in the schools it served.

Lickona (1991) reports on several successful character education initiatives. One of the most interesting was a systematic study done by the California Child Development Project and the Hewlett Foundation. This study examined a multifaceted values program in the San Marcos School District, asking, does the character education program work? Six elementary schools were used as experimental and control groups in this comprehensive study. The researchers systematically divided the experimental and control schools along socioeconomic and racial lines to ensure an objective study. Lickona reports that after 5 years of research the "report card was positive" in that statistically significant differences occurred in four areas: (a) classroom behavior, (b) playground behavior, (c) social problem-solving skills, and (d) commitment to democratic values. Moreover, Lickona reports, "These gains have been achieved without any sacrifice in academic achievement" (pp. 87-88).

In an earlier study, Kubelick (1976) established a "just community" at Falk Laboratory School at the University of Pittsburgh. Using small groups to promote discussion, strong teacher-student interactions, and the development of value-laden lessons with 8-, 9-, and 10-year-olds, the researcher emphasized to the students the importance of such traits as honesty, cooperation, trust, and determination. After systematically studying almost 100 children for one academic year, the researcher concluded that the children's behavior and attitudes toward themselves and others did improve. An independent report using the Iowa Tests of

Basic Skills demonstrated that academically the students in the Kube-lick study did as well as or better than other students in the school who did not participate in the character education project.

Allen School in Dayton, Ohio, was a haven for apathy, violence, and poor academic achievement. It was one of the lowest academically ranked schools in the Dayton school system and held the dubious distinction of consistently having one of the highest absentee and expulsion rates. In January 1989, Allen School welcomed its third principal of the year as the school seemed to be getting worse. The teachers, led by their new principal, Rudy Bernardo, went to work. They developed their own character education program to infuse the notion of values and good citizenship in every school program. They announced a "value of the week" and teachers would gear their lessons to that value. Responsibility, respect, cooperation, trust, and self-esteem were only a few of the values that teachers and students emphasized to rebuild a learning community in the school.

Everyone began to witness a slow but steady transformation. Discipline problems dropped off dramatically; absenteeism began to decline; and test scores, as measured by standardized instruments, began to increase. Today, Allen School is the top-ranked elementary school in the Dayton school system. It has one of the lowest absentee rates in the district and is touted as a model of what an urban school should be.

What happened at Allen School? As Charles Joiner, Jr. (1994), explains in a preface of a monograph that describes the transformation of Allen School, "He [the principal] empowered the teachers to create a value system. . . . It is important to note that this story involves three main elements: values-based leadership, systematic recognition of the importance of attitude and culture, and change in the structure of routine" (p. 109).

Joseph Gauld knows what makes a good school. Frustrated by an educational structure that focused only on academic growth, Gauld left the mainstream of education to found the Hyde School in Bath, Maine. Here, he crafted a learning environment based on character traits such as courage, integrity, leadership, curiosity, and concern for others. In his (1993) book *Character First: The Hyde School Experience*, Gauld chronicles his career in education and his triumph in developing a school that is built on the development of character, not only test results. As Gauld puts it, "If we want to transform American schools, our first imperative must be to communicate the following convictions to all American kids . . . that their true worth is measured, not by their social status, intellect, or talents, but by the strength of their character" (p. 168).

U.S. schools seem to be "waking up" to the clarion call for character education in our classrooms. Some urban public schools have adopted character education programs that range from the wearing of uniforms to the recitation of virtuous slogans to encourage self-esteem. One public school principal, Kenneth Barbour, who used this age-old approach in an elementary school in the Pittsburgh public schools reflected, "It's the only thing that does work! Problems in this school are down, and test scores are up."

CONCLUSION

What we describe as character development has long been a part of our schools. Character development in the earliest schools was the tool counted on to help bind together our communities in the relentless precolonial crusade against spiritual evil. Character development and its constituent values were relied on by our nation's founders to further concepts such as independence, responsibility, and self-reliance in our country's early beginnings. Character education fostered the great school movements of the 19th century and helped shape a formidable work ethic in a newly industrialized society. The development of character helped lay the groundwork for even the Progressive Era of education and the ideas we largely now use as a platform as we strive for social understanding and academic excellence.

Binding together this great U.S. school tradition of character education are any number of successful curricula. These range from a harsh and traditional approach such as recitation of virtuous poems or rules to more progressive approaches that employ discussion, literature, problem solving, discovery, participation, and action. Yet, they share the common goal of helping children discern right from wrong and foster a sense of individual responsibility to enhance society through thoughts and deeds. There is no one "silver bullet" for the problems that assault our schools. Moreover, we are beginning to realize that integrating character in the curriculum and daily lessons of the school may be the key to preparing our youth to meet the challenges of the next century.

―――――――――――――――●―――――――――――――――

REFERENCES

Beales, J. R., & Wahl, M. (1995). *Given the choice: A study of the PAVE program and school choice in Milwaukee* (Policy Study No. 183). Milwaukee, WI: The Reason Foundation.

Beauchamp, G. A. (1975). *Curriculum theory*. Wilmette, IL: Kagg.

Gauld, J. (1993). *Character first: The Hyde School experience*. San Francisco: Center for Self Governance.

Goodlad, J. I., & Richter, N., Jr. (1966). *The development of a conceptual system for dealing with problems of curriculum and instruction*. Los Angeles: Institute for Development of Educational Activities, University of California.

Joiner, C. W., Jr. (1994). *Building character schoolwide: The Allen School experience*. West Mifflin, PA: Your Environment Press.

Keen, E. (1975). *A primer in phenomenological psychology*. New York: University Press of America.

Knowles, R. T. (1992). The acting person as moral agent: Erikson as the starting point for an integrated psychological theory of moral development. In R. T. Knowles & G. F. McLean (Eds.), *Psychological foundation of moral education and character development*. Washington, DC: Council for Research in Values and Philosophy.

Krathwahl, D. R., Bloom, B. S., & Masia, B. B. (1967). *Taxonomy of educational objectives: The classification of educational goals. Handbook 11: Affective domain*. New York: David McKay.

Kubelick, C. (1976). *A study of the effects of a classroom intervention strategy on the cognitive moral development of eight, nine and ten year olds*. Unpublished doctoral dissertation, University of Pittsburgh.

Lickona, T. (1991). *Education for character: How our schools can teach respect and responsibility*. New York: Bantam.

McClellan, M. C. (1989, April). An interview with George Madus: New ways of thinking about testing. *Phi Delta Kappan*, pp. 642-645.

McLarin, K. J. (1995, February 11). Finding the great teachers. *New York Times*, p. 35.

McNeil, J. (1996). *Curriculum: A comprehensive introduction* (5th ed.). New York: HarperCollins.

Noddings, N. (1995, May). Teaching themes of care. *Phi Delta Kappan*, p. 676.

Personal Responsibility Education Process (PREP). (1995). *The Network for Educational Development—A division of the Cooperating School Districts*. St. Louis, MO: Author.

Project Essential Group. (1995). *Project Essential: A research study*. Edwing Marion Kauffman Foundation, 4900 Oak Street, Kansas City, MO.

Roosevelt, T. (1904). *State of the union address to Congress*.

Taba, H. (1971). The functions of a conceptual framework for curriculum design. In R. Hooper (Ed.), *The curriculum: Context, design and development*. Edinburgh: Oliver & Boyd.

Taylor, P. H., & Richards, C. M. (1985). *An introduction to curriculum studies.* Windsor, UK: NFER-Nelson.

Tyler, R. W. (1975). *Basic principles of curriculum and instruction.* Chicago: University of Chicago Press, 1975.

Wynne, E. A., & Ryan, K. (1993). *Reclaiming our schools.* New York: Merrill.

2

Making Character Work

WILLIAM J. SWITALA

Curriculum Director
Bethel Park School District
Bethel Park, Pennsylvania

"Intelligence plus character—that is the goal of a true education."

—Martin Luther King, Jr.

For more than 30 years, I have had the pleasure of helping the Bethel Park School District to become one of the finest examples of public education in the Pittsburgh region. Our elementary school teaching teams have worked tirelessly to adapt the most current innovations and programs to meet the needs of our youngsters. Our middle school is second to none and has received national awards for its superior programs. And, finally, I believe our high school program can compete with almost any secondary school in the country, challenging students with a range of courses that just a few years ago were offered only at the college level. The academic statistics speak for themselves, as over 85% of our students advance their education through technical or university training. I believe that much of our success lies in how we integrate character in the classrooms, activities, and general life of our schools.

We are typical of most suburban school systems in the region. Located 10 miles south of Pittsburgh, Pennsylvania, our population is a heterogeneous blend of economic groups ranging from old coal-mining communities to very affluent housing developments. The students come to the schools with diverse backgrounds, value systems, and attitudes. The staff of the system has always been cognizant of this diversity and has applied a host of strategies to meet students' needs. By almost any measure, our schools are a success and a true source of pride in the community.

Despite our achievements in the district, I am worried. I see more and more students begin kindergarten already bombarded by a world of distractions designed to lure them away from the educational tasks at hand, and in the process they disrespect adults, traditions, and institutions that have acted as the mortar of our culture. The assault increases in intensity and sophistication throughout their school careers. Video games, sound bites, MTV-type quick visual imagery, and a plethora of commercial seductions produce a mind-set in children and youth that demands instant gratification and makes the discipline of extended study in school or at home difficult at best.

We see the net result played out daily in schools across the country. For an increasing number of students, cheating has become a perfectly acceptable alternative to hard work. Intolerance, impatience, and disrespect are commonplace in most schools. There is a callous disregard for life and an ever-quickening tendency to settle disputes, however slight, with escalating violence. Peaceful resolution of conflicts is a skill that has not been taught to many children. The dignity of the individual and a sense of responsibility for one's actions are foreign to large numbers of young people. How can learning take place in an environment where one is fearful for one's safety?

KEYS TO SUCCESS

One of the keys to our success in the Bethel Park schools, I believe, lies in our efforts to integrate character in the daily routine of every school

in our district. We view character development as an important part of
the overall growth of each student in our district.

Each level in the system—elementary, middle, and high school—
has used techniques to foster positive qualities, such as honesty, trustworthiness, punctuality, cooperation, respect, and responsibility. This
has occurred through district- or school-sponsored programs as well as
through individual teacher efforts. I believe that the integration of character development in our schools has made a difference, one that may
be seen both academically and socially.

The elementary program teaches character in three major ways: individual teacher strategies and practices, extracurricular activities, and
schoolwide activities.

Janet Paterra, a master first-grade teacher in our system, has developed a particularly effective technique for fostering the value of respect
in younger students. The mainstay of her approach is continuous use
of positive reinforcement. Her method of reinforcing desirable behavior traits is to capitalize on every instance of a student demonstrating
respect, responsibility, and cooperation with others. In her classroom,
one frequently hears positive phrases such as, "I like the way Johnny is
sitting up so nice and straight," "Thank you for raising your hand before answering that question," and "Did everyone see how quietly
Mary sharpened her pencil so that she did not disturb anyone?" This
practice even continues on the playground during recess. "I like the
way Jimmy shared the swings" and "Did everyone notice how Ralph
played the game following all of the rules?" She also has students explain why they need to follow certain rules in the classroom. In the end,
Paterra's students demonstrate a whole host of positive character traits,
such as cooperation with their peers, respect, cooperation, and responsibility, due to her reinforcing techniques. It is very common for parents
to comment on how positively Paterra's classroom techniques have carried over in the daily lives of the children outside the classroom.

Fourth-grade teacher Carl Shipley uses a different strategy to foster
character development. Since his students are older, he works with his
students at the beginning of each year to develop a code of conduct. He
also gives each child a copy of the code to take home. "I give as much
attention to the affective domain as I do to the cognitive one," Shipley
states. The code contains a list of statements that are all couched in positive terms. There are no "Thou shalt not's." The list extends from "We
are kind, patient, and take turns" to "We have our assignments done on

time." Shipley feels that his code is effective for two reasons: "First, I am a role model for the class. I abide by the code at all times in my personal dealings with the students"; and second, the items of the code are all positive. "Negative statements often become challenges to students at this age level," Shipley holds. By the end of the first nine weeks of school, the vast majority of the class is following the code.

Carl Shipley is also our district coordinator for the Just Say No Clubs that operate in our middle and high schools. As Shipley notes, "The club teaches refusal skills in a positive way; they teach students how to say 'no,' not only to drugs and alcohol, but also to the temptations of cheating on exams, shoplifting, and how to avoid the potential for molestation situations." "The strength of the program lies in the way we reinforce the ideas of nonuse as the norm," Shipley adds. Positive character traits are fostered through an emphasis on personal responsibility for one's actions and the development of ethical decision-making skills through the Just Say No Clubs. The instructional component of the clubs is supplemented by numerous social activities. Picnics, boat rides, and trips to recreational areas help foster fellowship and provide an opportunity to reinforce desirable attitudes learned in the academic side of the program. Students, parents, and teachers have found this program to be both popular and effective.

Another method of fostering character development in our schools is seen in the Police Pals program. In this program one or two officers from the local police force form a special relationship with a particular school. The officers visit the school on a regular basis and attend most of the social functions conducted at the school. They even come and eat lunch with the students in the cafeteria and are an integral part of the Just Say No Club. All of this is done on a volunteer basis on each officer's own time. A major goal of this program is to foster a positive relationship between the student body and the police department. "Students have a good feeling about the role of the police in the community," states James Willison, an elementary principal in our district. Through the Police Pals program, students develop a better sense of the importance of laws as something designed for the common good than they would by simply studying about that concept in the classroom. Police officers are viewed now in a positive light as people who protect and help as opposed to individuals who forbid and suppress.

The effect of the Police Pals program has been extremely positive. Students and parents have commented on a renewed respect for police and their role in society. Moreover, the program has deepened an interest in the citizenship program in our schools, as students have come away from this experience with a better concept of citizenship and the traits necessary in becoming a good citizen.

COMMITMENT TO CHARACTER

Recently, the district adopted a comprehensive character development program. As a blueprint, the district used materials from the Jefferson Center for Character Education in Los Angeles, California. Each school began to systematically focus on a mutually agreed on series of desirable traits, such as honesty, reliability, respect, and cooperation, throughout each subject. Mark Hruska, a fifth-grade teacher, commented, "This approach blends in perfectly with our curriculum. It also supports the techniques I was already using in my classes to teach good character traits."

Many of the teachers who began this approach for the past school year have noted an improvement in student behavior. There were fewer fights on the playground, and students did their class assignments more efficiently more often. Michael Petrossi, a music teacher in the elementary schools, conducted a survey sampling teacher impressions of the approach. He found that 90% of teachers felt that this type of integration of positive character traits had produced a positive change in student attitude and behavior.

A basic character trait that teachers have always sought to develop is respect. John Reynolds, a veteran of more than 34 years of teaching at the elementary and middle school levels, has always stressed the development of this trait. When meeting his students at the beginning of the year, he emphasizes behavior that exemplifies mutual respect and continuously discusses and cites specific examples of respect to his classes throughout the year. The key to his success is that he models respect toward his students and his colleagues throughout the day. Now that he is part of an interdisciplinary team of five teachers who work with the same group of 130 students, he has convinced his colleagues to make respect a primary goal of their team. The result of this effort is seen in the marked improvement in class discipline. Fewer students need reprimands and the team has not referred anyone to the building office for principal action. Students bicker less and manifest greater respect for one another in the classroom.

The middle school in Bethel Park continues the development of character begun in the elementary schools. Independence Middle School, with an enrollment of approximately 1,100 students in Grades 6 through 8, has received the Presidential School of Excellence Award. The staff is child centered and eager to do whatever is needed for the intellectual and emotional development of the students who attend the school. Although the school abounds in innovative programs, three of them pertain directly to the development of desirable ethical and character traits in adolescents. These are the Advisor/Advisee, Community Service, and Character Education programs, which operate on a year-long basis.

The Advisor/Advisee program has been at Independence School for almost 10 years. Its primary goal is to provide small groups of youngsters with a specific adult member of the staff with whom they can interact on a more personal level. The program helps students share the perceptions, emotions, and frustrations faced by adolescents in and out of the school environment. At the heart of this approach is the opportunity provided to students to express their concerns and share common problems with their peers and a caring adult. Structured activities are conducted that help focus the students in their discussions. Many of these center students' attention on what it takes to succeed as a student and as a person. Punctuality, responsibility, conflict resolution, and honesty are some of the topics discussed. The assistant principal of the school, Carol Rosenfelder, believes the Advisor/Advisee Program is at the center of an effective middle school: "The Advisory program is integral to the middle school. It supports the transition youngsters must undergo moving from a small self-contained elementary classroom to the large setting of the multidiscipline curriculum in the middle school." Rosenfelder adds, "The Advisory program fosters positive traits such as cooperation, making choices, and accepting responsibility for making those choices. If we didn't have it, there would be a much greater level of disrespect here."

The second initiative that builds character at Independence Middle School is community service. Initiated 5 years ago by the principal of Independence, Robert David, the program is designed to offer students an opportunity to learn values, social skills, and a sense of responsibility, all of which are pertinent to fostering good citizenship. Community service at this age level teaches the fundamental skills of collaboration, problem solving, and conflict resolution. To accomplish these desirable traits, David has structured a program that involves service projects both in the school setting and in the community. In the school, students serve as peer tutors, lab assistants, safety officers, and members of school government bodies. Outside the school, student activities include assisting in child care, helping handicapped individuals, making baskets of flowers and gifts for nursing homes, environmentally oriented cleanup campaigns, and fund-raising for local charities. While engaging in these activities, students are made aware of the challenges facing their community and the nation as a whole, they learn to recognize that they have power to improve their world through personal involvement, and they develop a sense of personal fulfillment through their contributions.

The final ingredient in the process of personal development of the students at the middle school is a formal character education program. Like the elementary level, the middle school uses a comprehensive character-building approach in each subject. The teachers, however, have expanded on the method and are adding a component on peer mediation and conflict resolution. Betsy Ranick, a reading teacher at the middle school and a member of the district's character education committee, has seen the impact that this program has made on student behavior: "I have noted a marked improvement in student interactions, courtesy, and overall behavior since we began," says Ranick. "Students are developing a much greater sense of responsibility for their actions. They are completing their homework assignments on time, they are bickering less, cheating has disappeared, and politeness has returned in my classroom."

The idea of developing student character is a constant theme in our middle school. Individual and groups of teachers used a variety of techniques in their classrooms long before any formal programs began.

A pair of home economics teachers have always viewed politeness and proper behavior in social settings as critical features in the character development of adolescents. Marianne Bricker and Nancy Nawrocki were concerned with the lack of common courtesy, especially the deplorable table manners they witnessed middle-level students display in the school, the cafeteria, and restaurants. To help remedy the situation, they decided to weave proper dining etiquette and polite behavior into their home economics classes. In the unit on cooking in the curriculum, they include dining simulations where polite and proper eating etiquette is modeled and practiced by their students. Students must work in pairs in the cooking lab and the teachers constantly reinforce polite interactions between the partners. Both teachers admit to being surprised at how successfully the program has operated. Students actually showed a real interest in learning proper table manners. Many admitted that they had never learned how to use eating utensils properly. Simple procedures such as the correct way to hold a knife and fork when cutting food, unfolding a napkin on one's lap, and the polite way of asking that food or condiments be passed were a revelation for some students. Above all else, the teachers have noted an improvement in politeness and courtesy among the students in their daily interactions in the classroom.

Albert Lebedda, a social studies teacher at Independence, uses another technique to promote a sense of responsibility in his students. A veteran with more than 35 years of teaching experience, Lebedda employs the cooperative learning technique known as Think-Pair-Share to teach responsibility. He pairs students of varying academic abilities and stresses the need for them to help one another in the process of learning new material. As the pair works together, the more academically talented student begins to develop a sense of responsibility for ensuring that his or her partner is learning the materials. The results of this technique are twofold. First, both students demonstrate a better understanding of the lesson. The student doing the tutoring knows the material better by virtue of having to explain it to another, and the student being tutored knows it better because the explanation was done at a more understandable level due to the fact that a peer has done the explaining. Second, character traits such as caring and personal responsibility are fostered.

Character development at the high school follows lines similar to those of the elementary and middle schools. Individual teachers establish standards in their classrooms. Courses such as American history, American government, humanities, democratic leadership, and the law and you stress positive citizenship traits as part of their curricula. Finally, there is an established discipline program, known as "responsibility training," in force for the entire school.

Responsibility training improves discipline at Bethel Park High School. This system derives its basic components from William Glasser's (1986) "control theory." Essentially, the goals of the program, according to Lawrence Bukowski, principal of the high school, are "to develop a sense of individual responsibility in students, more cooperation between teachers and students, and to bring about a better understanding of the consequences for personal actions." The operating procedure for the program is quite simple. All teachers review a standard set of rules related to behavior and procedures with the classes they teach. If a student violates one of the classroom management rules, the teacher acknowledges it with a verbal proscription. If the behavior persists, the student is isolated in the classroom. If even that fails to correct poor behavior, the student is sent to the "time out" room. This is a classroom staffed by a teacher trained in the intricacies of the program. The student remains in this room until he or she develops a written plan for behavior modification. Bukowski comments, "I can honestly say that I have witnessed far less confrontation between teachers and students since we began the program." Teachers' reaction to this initiative has been positive. They state that after a trip to the time-out room students are much better behaved in the class and are more cooperative.

Many teachers at the high school level have used a whole host of techniques and activities to build on the development of character education. Some of those techniques have an element of culmination to them in that they sum up all the efforts spent by previous teachers to bring about a positive moral and ethical attitude in students as they progress though the school system. An excellent example of a culminating activity can be seen in an exercise developed by Ronald Teitz for high school seniors.

Teitz is a veteran of many years of teaching social studies at Bethel Park High School. In his humanities class, which is designed for seniors, he concludes the course with a final 9-week unit on ethics. Students read and discuss theories of several ethical systems. To motivate his students to think deeply about their own ethical attitudes, Teitz has developed a research activity in which students choose from one of four contemporary areas involving ethical decision making and research the ethical problems found in their particular choice. They must develop a portfolio of their findings and it must include an analysis of their own ethical perspectives in this area. In this way, each student is forced to focus on his or her own ethical and moral views of life. For most students, this is the first time they have ever gone though self-examination of this nature.

Former students continuously comment on the value of this exercise. They see that their professions are more than a process of going to work—real ethical decisions must be considered in order to create a better workplace, employ factual knowledge, and make decisions that affect people's lives.

————————●————————

THE IMPORTANCE OF CHARACTER

In the Bethel Park schools, we believe that the power of knowledge can be harnessed only by fostering the growth of the whole child. By developing a supportive school environment and integrating classroom lessons that promote a sense of respect, responsibility, and cooperation, we are helping to produce academically talented and socially responsible citizens. Our students are knowledgeable, but they are armed with a sense of values—a powerful tool that helps them use their knowledge constructively. This is why, I believe, we are so successful in the Bethel Park schools. By integrating character in the life of our school, we are confident that our students can compete with the best students in the nation and the world.

————————●————————

REFERENCE

Glasser, W. (1986). *Control theory in the classroom.* New York: HarperCollins.

Principle Two

Integrated Character Education Is Action Education

3

Character, Curriculum, and Action Education

THOMAS FARRELLY

Professor Emeritus, Duquesne University

"I am convinced that we must train not only the head, but the heart and hand as well."

—Madame Chiang Kai-shek

There are two main schools of thought regarding the proper focus of character education. One school of thought focuses on the person and emphasizes factors such as moral reasoning and dispositions. The other school of thought focuses on the environment and emphasizes factors such as culture and norms. The integrated approach to character education regards these two positions as complementary and shifts the focus of attention to the sphere of interaction between the person and the environment. This interactionist emphasis directs the attention of educators to the living experience of moral action itself, in which affectivity, reasoning, and environmental influences are inextricably mingled.

The integrated approach endeavors to restore due emphasis to the role of affectivity in moral education because of its importance in moral action. To act morally, I need both to be convinced intellectually of the rightness of an act and to be attracted by its goodness. A person of mature moral character is attracted by what is good and repulsed by what is evil.

The purpose of the present chapter is to present a rationale for curriculum planning appropriate for integrated character education. The first part of the chapter presents a rationale for curriculum planning based on the philosophical, psychological, and social foundations of integrated character education. The second part of the chapter briefly outlines a process for developing an integrated character education curriculum supported by this rationale.

A RATIONALE FOR INTEGRATED CHARACTER EDUCATION

In the integrated model of character education, character means, "that in us which patterns our actions in a relatively fixed way." Although educators cannot teach character directly, they can create favorable conditions for its development and can teach appropriate knowledge, skills, and appreciations. The term *integrated* refers both to curriculum integration and to personality integration (Nicgorski & Ellrod, 1986, p. 142).

The psychological foundations of integrated character education owe much to Erik Erikson's (1963) theory of psychosocial development, as broadened by Knowles (1992). In the Erikson-Knowles paradigm, moral action is conceptualized as a bipolar interaction between a "subject pole" (the person) and an "object pole" (the environment) within a horizon of values. This conceptualization differs from that of some other modern theories, such as behaviorism, which emphasize reaction to the environment rather than interaction with it. The present theory gives the person a more proactive role in moral action.

The subject pole (the person) thus represents the three main aspects of personality: the vital, the cognitive, and the self aspects. The vital aspect includes both the bodily and affective components (Knowles, 1992).

The object pole represents the environment with which the person interacts, which includes three systems. Other human beings constitute the social system in the environment, the world constructed by human beings constitutes the cultural system, and the world of nature and the physical world constitute the ecological system (Pegoraro, 1989). Moral action therefore involves interaction with the social, cultural, and ecological systems in the environment.

The expression "horizon of values" indicates that the person-environment interaction has a moral dimension, because it is seen by the acting person in a values context. *Horizon* is used here in the sense of the background or context that gives meaning to our activities.

The integrated approach to character education recognizes that the ability to act morally is developmental. Erikson's psychosocial theory, as broadened by Knowles (1992), describes moral development as a lifelong process in seven stages from the first year of life to older adulthood.

Childhood	Trust versus mistrust	Hope
	Autonomy versus shame and doubt	Will
	Industry versus inferiority	Purpose
Adulthood	Identity versus role diffusion	Commitment
	Intimacy versus isolation	Loving
	Generativity versus stagnation	Caring
	Integrity versus despair	Wisdom

Each stage is characterized by an ego crisis and a virtue that is achieved when the crisis is successfully resolved. Each virtue represents a strength of the self. The above outline shows the ego crisis and virtue at each stage in childhood and adulthood (Erikson, 1963).

Ralph Tyler (1949), often referred to as the father of U.S. curriculum theory, recommended that curriculum should be based on philosophy, on the empirical study of the society, and on educational research (Tyler, 1949). The foundations of integrated character education have already been described in these categories in several publications, many of which are listed in the references at the end of this chapter. The rationale presented here is a summary statement of these foundations.

Four dimensions of character development provide guidelines for program planning (Knowles, 1988) and serve to underline the differences between the integrated approach to character education and other approaches: (1) character develops through moral action; (2) character develops through interaction with the social, cultural, and natural environments; (3) character integrates the whole personality; and (4) character shows consistent patterns of action and values. The contributions of philosophy, psychology, and sociology are considered in relation to each dimension.

1. Character Develops Through Moral Action

A philosophical foundation for the statement *Character develops through moral action* is offered by McLean (1986), who draws attention to the connection between moral action and character development. He points out that in acting freely I experience myself as wholly engaged in an action that is my own and for which I am responsible. As part of me, my action either promotes or retards my moral development: "In making choices which shape my world I form also myself for good or evil" (p. 384). As McLean also points out, it is only morally good actions—actions identified as good by one's conscience—that contribute to character development and self-fulfillment (p. 389).

Knowles, writing from a psychological perspective, asserts that the decisive point about the integrated model of character development is that it is a theory of moral action rather than of moral thought (1992, p. 222). It is through moral action that people express their values and create society and culture (De Piazza, 1989, p. 43). It is important to note that "action" may in fact involve a decision not to act, as in a case where someone is being coerced to act contrary to his or her conscience.

The educational setting should allow students to confront real moral problems in the school and community; to propose imaginative solutions for them; and, if possible, to engage in action to implement those solutions (Knowles, 1992, p. 248). Other approaches to moral education stop at moral reasoning or clarification of students' values. Integrated character education offers opportunities not only for moral thinking but for moral action, which is seen as essential for character development.

2. Character Develops Through Interaction

Pegoraro (1989) underlines the fact that personal development takes place in the context of interaction with the social, cultural, and natural environments. I am not independent of my environments. Even if I live alone in a cave and survive on wild berries, I am still dependent on the natural environment. If I want to live among other humans, however, I must share their values and culture. This is one reason why it is illusory to hold that I am completely free to choose my values, as if they were flavors of ice cream. If I am to develop as a human being, I need to share the values of my society and culture, while retaining the right to reject any value that is inimical to human freedom and development.

The person today is understood as a human being living in relation with other persons who, in turn, are related to nature and culture. This means that the person in his or her own interiority is incomplete: "The notion of person must be completed by relationships to other persons and to the community" (Pegoraro, 1989, p. 5).

Knowles (1992) notes from a psychological perspective, based on Erikson's (1963) developmental theory, that the effect of moral action is twofold. In the social environment, a value (justice, truth, etc.), is advanced. In the acting person, there is enhancement of the self, called "virtue" (p. 222). From a sociological standpoint, people create their culture in light of their values. The culture in turn influences people and their value development (De Piazza, 1989, p. 46). The relativist stance that values are purely subjective is not borne out by experience. De Piazza points out that values are objectified and built into cultures which may have just and unjust elements in them.

Consequently, a character education program needs to give students opportunities to learn the values of their society and culture and to learn to critique their society and culture in light of its own higher values. They also need to be able to participate creatively in the positive moral values in their social, cultural, and natural environments. In this way, they come to learn that society does not exist for their benefit only, but that they owe it something in return and that it needs their contribution. Community service projects, school activities, and a participatory learning environment provide opportunities for such creative participation.

3. Character Integrates the Whole Personality

The excessive intellectualist emphasis of much moral education has led to a neglect of affectivity. By *affectivity* is meant not just emotions such as fear or anger, which are modifications of psychological states, but the deeper value orientations such as trust, respect, courage, and caring that emanate from the self and supply the dynamism for moral action. Integrated character education attempts to help students to achieve a balanced development of cognition, affectivity, and emotional response.

From a philosophical standpoint, it can be argued that there is a need for a harmonious and balanced integration of all dimensions of the personality. No one can continue to exist as a war zone of conflicting desires, decisions, and emotions. To be truly free and self-determining, "The person must not merely moderate a bargaining session between will, body and psyche, but constitute a new and active dynamism in which all dimensions achieve their properly personal character" (McLean, 1986, p. 387).

Looking at personality integration from a psychological viewpoint, Knowles (1992, p. 224) identifies the self as the integrating force for the other two aspects of personality: the vital (including both the physical and the affective) and the cognitive.

Brabeck and Gorman (1992, p. 89) describe how cognition and the emotions work together to instigate, evaluate, or inhibit moral behavior. Social psychologists remind us that both personality variables and environmental factors influence moral action (Leone & Graziano, 1992, p. 185).

Activities and experiences provided by the school should be designed to foster growth toward the harmonious integration by the self of the physical, affective, and cognitive dimensions of the personality, resulting in a self-confident individual capable of moral action—what has been traditionally known as "education of hand, heart, and head."

4. Character Shows Consistency

Philosophers stress that if moral action is to foster progress toward moral maturity, it should not be capricious or intermittent but should exhibit stable patterns called *virtues*. To be dignified with the title "virtue," a pattern of action should be more than a routine habit or a reflex action. It should be consciously motivated by positive values. McLean (1986) links moral development with virtues and values by asserting, "Moral development as a process of personal maturation consists in bringing my pattern of personal and social virtues into harmony with corresponding sets of values" (p. 390).

Knowles (1992), following the Eriksonian paradigm, links consistency to the identity crisis of adolescence, which involves the movement toward adult love and commitment. "In this broader understanding the virtues of adulthood are constituted by loving and caring for the projects and people in our calling. Obviously, for such caring to be effective some basic consistency is necessary" (p. 244).

Musser and Leone (1992, p. 152) point out that regularity in behavior across time and setting is considered by some to be prima facie evidence for the existence and impact of character.

The character education curriculum should be designed to help students grow in the ability to act consistently and to freely commit themselves to a set of positive values, the objective worth of which may be rationally shown but which nonetheless require an act of free acceptance from the student.

This discussion of the four dimensions of character development in light of their philosophical, psychological, and sociological sources provides a framework and criteria for goal setting and program planning for integrated character education.

CURRICULUM PLANNING FOR INTEGRATED CHRACTER EDUCATION

Curriculum planning is defined by Beauchamp (1975) as "the substance and organization of goals and culture content" (p. 196). The process of curriculum planning is conceptualized as consisting of four activities: goal setting, curriculum design, instructional design, and evaluation design. For a more extended treatment of curriculum planning for integrated character education, see Rusnak, Farrelly, and Burrett (1992).

1. Goal Setting

The first suggested step in curriculum planning is goal setting. A set of goals for integrated character education based on the interactionist rationale for moral action outlined above is presented in Table 3.1. The overall goal is moral maturity through moral action. Since moral action is conceptualized as interaction between person and environment, there are two main categories of goals leading to moral maturity. Personal development goals relate to the person side of the interaction and sociocultural goals relate the environment side of the interaction. Each of these two categories is further subdivided, as in Table 3.1.

It is important to remember that when our focus is on either set of goals, the other set must also be kept in mind, since it represents the

Table 3.1 The Goals of Integrated Character Education

Overall Goal	The student, through moral action, becomes a person of mature moral character.

1. Personal Development Goals
a. Development of the Self

Childhood	The student develops openness, confidence, and self-reliance in moral action.
Adolescence	The student develops the ability to be faithful and caring in work and relationships.

b. Cognitive Development

Intellectual	The student develops the capacity for making moral judgments.
Self-Concept	The student becomes a self-aware and self-accepting person in relation to others.
View of Others	The student develops the capacity to be aware of others, their feelings, and their situation.
Transcendence	The student develops a vision or ideal of the meaning of life in light of which he/she makes moral choices.

c. Vital Development

Physical	The student develops a mature sense of sexual and physical identity as a component of full human identity.
Affective	The student becomes sensitized in moral matters to feel attracted by good and repulsed by evil.

2. Sociocultural Goals

Social	The student contributes creatively to the ongoing realization of moral values in the social environment.
Cultural	The student contributes creatively to the ongoing realization of moral values in the cultural environment.
Ecological	The student contributes creatively to the ongoing realization of moral values in interactions with the natural environment.

other side of the interaction. The goals have been deliberately formulated in broad terms so that they can be defined more precisely according to the needs of the students.

Valuable assistance in articulating these goals has been derived from the rationale developed by Knowles (1992) and from the synthesis presented by Gorman (1992, p. 267). It should be noted that Gorman includes self-concept under the cognitive aspect rather than under the self aspect. She also adds an important component, "view of the transcendent." Religious and other transcendent ideals play an important role in character development because of their power to motivate people.

2. Curriculum Design

The second suggested step in curriculum planning is curriculum design. This involves the organization of content in the form of themes related to the goals. Character education lends itself to thematic treatment, since moral virtues, values, and issues provide many themes. The categories of goals presented in Table 3.1 provide a framework to guide the process of selecting and organizing themes to ensure systematic coverage of all important areas of character education and avoid random selection of themes. One source of themes is Erikson's typology of virtues associated with the stages of development referred to above, such as hope, trust, and caring.

An important consideration when selecting themes is to select those that can be integrated in several subject areas. In science, mathematics, and technical subjects, themes can be generated by considering how the area in question enters into human interaction in our modern culture. For example, the question, "How do people use and misuse mathematics?" will suggest several themes, such as honesty and justice. The choice of themes should be made by a program development team involving teachers and curriculum specialists. Input from parents and community leaders may also be incorporated at this stage.

3. Instructional Design

The third suggested step in curriculum planning is the development of teaching units related to the themes previously selected at the curriculum design stage. Three aspects of instructional design that need to be considered are integration, scope, and sequence (Taba, 1971, p. 141). One key to integrating character education in the curriculum is considering how each subject contributes to the development of the student's character. In *The Mindful School: How to Integrate the Curricula*, Robin Fogarty (1991) offers 10 models for curriculum integration.

The problem of scope is that of deciding what is to be covered or learned. The scope of a curriculum is already partly addressed by the selection of themes. It is further addressed by determining the number of units to be assigned to a theme and the characteristics of the subject areas or aspects of school organization with which character education is being integrated.

The problem of sequence is an issue of continuity through grade levels, avoiding both lack of connectedness and undue repetition. It is necessary to give students a sense of progress so that they do not get the impression that they have been "through all this before" as a theme is developed vertically through grade levels. The rationale proposed by Gorman (1992, p. 267) provides a suitable framework for both scope and sequence. The process of instructional design is likely to be most effective when teachers work with curriculum specialists in interdisciplinary teams to ensure coordination of themes across subject areas.

4. Evaluation and Modification

The fourth suggested step in curriculum planning is evaluation and modification of the program. The type of program envisaged here is not a set of separate courses but a plan to integrate character education in all aspects of the curriculum. Evaluation of student progress in character development is greatly facilitated by two features of the integrated approach: the emphasis on moral action and the articulation of a set of developmental goals.

Moral action is usually observable and lends itself to the determination of identifiable knowledge, skills, and appreciations. Although it is true that not all aspects of character development are observable, moral action is an important aspect that is observable. The developmental goals provide criteria for evaluations of different age levels. The main consideration is assessing the degree to which the goals of the program are being met, which can be monitored continually if an evaluation element is built into each unit. A good example of this approach, involving both quantitative and qualitative assessment, is given by Shoemaker and Lewin (1993).

Recent years have seen a shift in focus in evaluation from quantitative methods to qualitative methods (Stake, 1991). Cline and Feldmesser (1983) provide guidelines for the use of quantitative evaluation methods with moral education programs. Qualitative methods appear to agree well with the person-centered approach of integrated character education, which favors the description of experiences in active situations rather than pencil-and-paper tests (Bogdan & Biklen, 1992; Eisner, 1991; Patton, 1987).

The aim of the integrated approach to character education is to help the student to grow toward maturity of character. In this process, the development of curriculum enables the teacher to grow professionally by participating in every stage of the process of developing a program based on sound theoretical and research foundations.

REFERENCES

Beauchamp, G. A. (1975). *Curriculum theory.* Wilmette, IL: Kagg.

Bogdan, R. C., & Biklen, S. K. (1992). *Qualitative research for education: An introduction to theory and methods.* Boston: Allyn & Bacon.

Brabeck, M., & Gorman, M. (1992). Emotions and morality. In R. T. Knowles & G. F. McLean (Eds.), *Psychological foundations of moral education and character development* (2nd ed.). Washington, DC: Council for Research in Values and Philosophy.

Cline, H. F., & Feldmesser, R. A. (1983). *Program evaluation in moral education.* Princeton, NJ: Educational Testing Service.

De Piazza, H. F. (1989). Values in an historical, socio-cultural context. In G. F. McLean & O. Pegoraro (Eds.), *The social context and values: Perspectives of the Americas.* New York: University Press of America.

Eisner, E. S. (1991). Taking a second look: Educational connoisseurship revisited. In M. W. McLaughlin & D. C. Phillips (Eds.), *Evaluation and education at quarter century: Ninetieth yearbook of the National Society for the Study of Education. Part 2.* Chicago: University of Chicago Press.

Erikson, E. H. (1963). *Childhood and society.* (35th ed.). New York: Norton.

Fogarty, R. (1991). *The mindful school: How to integrate the curricula.* Palatine, IL: IRI Skylight.

Gorman, M. (1992). Life-long moral development. In R. T. Knowles & G. F. McLean (Eds.), *Psychological foundations for moral education and character development* (2nd ed.). Washington, DC: Council for Research in Values and Philosophy.

Knowles, R. T. (1988). *A summary of the moral education project developed by the Council for Research in Values and Philosophy.* Unpublished paper delivered at the 1988 Annual Conference of the Association for Moral Education, Pittsburgh, PA.

Knowles, R. T. (1992). The acting person as moral agent: Erikson as the starting point for an integrated psychological theory of moral development. In R. T. Knowles & G. F. McLean (Eds.), *Psychological foundations of moral education and character development* (2nd ed.). Washington, DC: Council for Research in Values and Philosophy.

Leone, C., & Graziano, W. The social environment and moral action. In R. T. Knowles & G. F. McLean (Eds.), *Psychological foundations of moral education and character development* (2nd ed.). Washington, DC: Council for Research in Values and Philosophy.

McLean, G. F. (1986). The person, moral growth, and character developoment. In G. F. McLean, F. E. Ellrod, D. Schindler, & J. Mann (Eds.), *Act and agent: Philosophical foundations for moral education and character development*. Washington, DC: University Press of America.

Musser, L. M., & Leone, C. (1992). Moral character: A social learning perspective. In R. T. Knowles & G. F. McLean (Eds.), *Psychological foundations of moral education and character development* (2nd ed.). Washington, DC: Council for Research in Values and Philosophy.

Nicgorski, W., & Ellrod, F. E. (1986). Moral character. In G. F. McLean, F. E. Ellrod, D. Schindler, & J. Mann (Eds.), *Act and agent: Philosophical foundations for moral education and character development*. Washington, DC: University Press of America.

Patton, M. Q. (1987). *How to use qualitative methods of evaluation.* Newbury Park, CA: Sage.

Pegoraro, O. (1989). Ethics and historicity. In G. F. McLean & O. Pegoraro (Eds.), *The social context and values: Perspectives of the Americas.* New York: University Press of America.

Rusnak, T., Farrelly, T., & Burrett, K. (1992). The integrated approach to character education. In T. Lickona & K. Ryan (Eds.), *Character development in schools and beyond.* Washington, DC: Council for Research in Values and Philosophy.

Shoemaker, B. J. R., & Lewin, L. (1993). Curriculum and assessment: Two sides of the same coin. *Educational Leadership,* pp. 55-57.

Stake, R. E. (1991). Retrospective on "The countenance of educational evaluation." In M. W. McLaughlin & D. C. Phillips (Eds.), *Evaluation and education at quarter century: Ninetieth yearbook of the National Society for the Study of Education. Part 2.* Chicago: University of Chicago Press.

Taba, H. (1971). The functions of a conceptual framework for curriculum design. In R. Hooper (Ed.), *The curriculum: Context, design and development.* Edinburgh: Oliver & Boyd.

Tyler, R. W. (1949). *Basic principles of curriculum and instruction.* Chicago: University of Chicago Press.

4

Learning Beyond the Classroom

JAMES ANTIS

Principal, Horace Mann Elementary School
Indiana, Pennsylvania

"We need to help children develop nobility. By nobility, I mean doing the right thing for the right reason. I think this can be taught just as we teach arithmetic or reading or biology."

—Jonas Salk

My school is a neighborhood school. It is located in a community where the majority of children walk to and from school, often accompanied by a parent. The school is a major part of family life and strongly supported by parental involvement. There is a positive identity associated with being a Horace Mann student and a neighborhood loyalty to school connections. The PTA is strong and actively involved in providing special events and activities that would not otherwise be available for our students. On any evening when there is a school- or PTA-sponsored activity, the building is filled with children, parents, grandparents, teachers, and others who have an interest in the children and life of the school. A few of our teachers, many of our parents, and even some of our grandparents were once students at Horace Mann School, so there is a rich history for many at the school. The facility is old, but it has a certain personality or character of its own. The school has an enduring presence in the neighborhood and the support staff maintains the physical plant from a position of pride that enhances the caring environment within.

We are fortunate to have a very dedicated and caring faculty. We have few real disciplinary problems and our students perform well academically due to the dedication of faculty and parents who are committed to instilling the value of learning and to nurturing the school environment. We have the typical problems associated with any school and we experience similar problems related to changes in family and society, but, all in all, Horace Mann School is a good place.

Societal values have gradually deteriorated in recent times and this change has had an effect on the moral development and ethical behavior of our children. I have read the articles and seen news broadcasts about schools in crisis whose leaders are seeking new programs to restore traditional values and bring a renewed interest in learning. Public awareness about these societal concerns has spawned a renewed interest in the need to instill traditional values in our children, thus generating a growing interest in character education programs.

-----------------●-----------------

CONTINUOUS IMPROVEMENT

Our school is not in crisis and the influence of traditional values remains present in our community. The schools I read and hear about in other places often appear desperate and are reaching out to character education as a last attempt to salvage a ray of hope for their children. For our purposes, character education has provided a means to ensure the preservation of our school's positive climate through a purposeful effort to teach children what is morally and ethically right, along with what is academically important in their development. It is not a mission to save a decaying environment but a means to enhance what was already positive about the school.

When I arrived at Horace Mann School as principal, it was evident that it was a good school, but not to the extent that there was no room for improvement. I established a program of continuous improvement that would address any issues of concern. Although things were good, I believed something could be done to improve the way we served children and the community. There was no lack of direction in the sense of not knowing what or how to teach children but perhaps in the sense of our ability as a professional staff to focus on other issues that cannot always be captured in the finest of academic programs. We needed a community within, a community of learners where parents, teachers, and students would share not only the joy of learning but also a sense of fulfillment from working together for a common cause.

When I began my doctoral study in 1993 at Duquesne University in Pittsburgh, Pennsylvania, I became a member of a unique program built around a cohort model that emphasized community, cooperation, and action learning. The approach was different from that of more traditional doctoral programs in that the community existed to develop educational leaders and support a mutual interest in learning that would have an impact on the educational community at large. As I had a lifelong interest in the area of ethics and decision making and had worked with children and young people for 28 years, it was not difficult for me to choose a dissertation topic related to ethics and moral development. The Center for Character Education, Civic Responsibility, and Teaching at Duquesne became a resource in helping to establish a direction for my research.

It soon became evident to me that character education could be a powerful tool to bring focus to our overall program at Horace Mann Elementary and collectively change our school to a unified community of learners. It was also clearly evident that character education would be the catalyst to foster a different kind of learning that would transcend the regular curriculum. It became the nucleus that moved us from being only a good school to becoming a great school.

THE BEGINNINGS

As part of our newly established program of continuous improvement, a quality circle comprising myself and a few faculty members was established to begin developing a strategy to monitor and enhance our character education program. It was obvious that the character-related concepts needed to be integrated in all that we did in the daily life of the school. This integrated approach, along with role modeling of the concepts, began to unify our school for common purpose. It was critical to establish the importance of crossing the gap from learning and understanding character-related concepts to placing this learning into action.

We began using a kit-type approach that would best serve our immediate needs. This quickly established the program as an integral component of our instructional process. The Heartwood Institute's (1993) character education curriculum was selected as it was a known and proven approach to teaching ethical concepts. It is a multicultural, literature-based ethics program intended for kindergarten through Grade 6. It includes a geography component and an extension activity for parents and focuses on the character-related concepts of hope, honesty, respect, loyalty, love, justice, and courage. It was attractive also in the sense that it could be incorporated in our existing language arts curriculum and not remain a separate entity from our existing program of instruction.

Following an inservice training, we implemented the program. My doctoral research simultaneously evaluated the effect of the program on the ethical understanding, ethical sensibility, and ethical behavior of the students. To clarify, *ethical understanding* refers to students' knowledge of the character-related attributes mentioned previously, *ethical sensibility* to the extent to which students express a preference for actions that exemplify the character traits, and *ethical behavior* to the social or conduct-related dimensions of character-related behavior. This can also be illustrated by visualizing the head, or the cognitive component; the heart, or the feeling about what is right; and the hands, or the acting out of the learned concepts. The difficulty is always translating learning to action and, therefore, this became the focus of our efforts. The program met with success and the culture of the school changed as learned character-related concepts began to reveal themselves in student behavior.

UNCONDITIONAL SUCCESS

As the concepts of character were incorporated into our language arts curriculum, a progression of our efforts led to related activities intended to integrate these concepts into the daily life of the school. Some of these initiatives were developed schoolwide and others were generated at the classroom or individual grade level. Some examples of what happened follow.

Lynn Clark and Maureen Busche, first-grade teachers, designed a class project focused on the character-related attribute of respect. The attribute was introduced to first-grade students through use of the literature and a related extension activity. *Miss Rumphius,* by Barbara Cooney Porter, is a story of a young girl and her journey from adulthood to her elderly years. Throughout her life, she strives to travel about the world, to live by the sea, and to make the world more beautiful. In this story, Miss Rumphius decides to beautify the world by planting lupines wherever she goes. Consequently, the members of her community also develop a desire for beauty in their world and learn the meaning of respect through Miss Rumphius's actions.

After reading the story, the children discussed the meaning of respect. The story of Miss Rumphius emphasized respect for the young and old, respect for the earth, self-respect, and pride in doing a job well. Following this story and discussion, the children were eager to plan a way to make their world more beautiful. Many ideas were generated. It was decided to plant lupines on the school property, not only to beautify our environment, but to remind us of the lessons of respect that Miss Rumphius had taught us.

To accomplish the task, the first graders invited the fourth-grade students to assist with the planting. Cooperatively, the student partners planned, planted, and cared for their designated area of the school grounds. The following spring when the lupines bloomed, both grades reunited for a second reading of *Miss Rumphius* while sitting alongside the flowers they had planted in the fall. This warm story, in addition to the observable beauty of the flowers, reinforced the values of respecting the earth, other people, and ourselves.

In the fourth grade, classroom teacher Deborah Sorce focused an activity on the character attribute of love. One of the stories exemplifying the attribute of love in the Heartwood curriculum is *The Rag Coat* by Lauren Mills. In this moving story, a poor Appalachian girl is given a quilted patchwork coat. Each patch was made from the rags of her schoolmates' old clothes and blankets. Through the memory of her gentle father and his gift, the girl learns to love in spite of experiencing poverty and prejudice. In turn, her schoolmates also learn a lesson in love and respect from this brave little girl.

Even though this story sent a powerful message to Sorce's students, it took place nearly 50 years ago. Sorce wanted to find a way to bring it to the present, to make it meaningful to her fourth graders. Obtaining information from the Christian Appalachian Project (CAP), she was able to bring to light the plight of children who live in the Appalachian mountains. On hearing some of the stories of children living in chicken coops and sheds, the immediate response from her students was shock and disbelief. After all, people don't live like that in our country, or at least no one thought they did!

A discussion followed about how a special stuffed animal or blanket gave each of the students a feeling of love and security when they were younger. Some students still had their security blanket or teddy today. They all agreed that no child should go without that "necessity" and wanted to make stuffed animals for these Appalachian children. Their concern extended to the fact that many of these children did not even have the luxury of having their own bed. They wanted the animals to be large enough to serve as pillows as well as pals! Tying the Appalachian theme to the story of the patchwork coat, the class decided to make stuffed patchwork animal pillows for the needy children of Appalachia.

The students were very excited about their project and felt a sense of ownership as they began to plan their pillow project. Through the generosity of many families, the class had more than enough donated material of every color and texture. The students were particular about which material they chose for their animals. After cutting 3-inch × 3-inch patches, the students placed their material patches, along with a pattern drawn on graph paper, in separate reusable plastic bags. They took these bags home to the many volunteer mothers, grandmothers, and teachers, who tirelessly sewed over 5,000 square yards of material together while following the patterns drawn by the students.

When all the pillows were sewn, the children had an in-class stuffing party. Twenty bags of polyester stuffing donated by local merchants and parents were used to stuff the animal pillows. The children painstakingly stitched the openings closed and added a few small details to their animals. Looking at the finished products, the students gleamed with pride at their accomplishment. Several students took their animals home to show their parents before sending them away.

When the boxes of patchwork pillows were filled, some of the students wanted to help these less fortunate children even more. Learning that CAP was in the process of creating a day care center but desperately in need of funds and equipment, the students launched a schoolwide collection campaign. They decorated a special box and asked for donations of toys and books appropriate for small children at a day care center. The children also took bonus points earned from their book club and purchased several new educational toys and supplies. When everything was packed, there were 15 large boxes stuffed with the children's gifts of love. The students were quite impressed by the massive collection. Through a contribution of the PTA, the children were able to send their gifts to a poverty area of Kentucky where members of CAP distributed the pillows to the young children of the area.

To quote Deborah Sorce,

> I was in awe of the enthusiasm of our students and the generosity of our parents. Throughout this program of fostering values growth, we were able not only to read about someone else's demonstration of love and understanding, but had the opportunity to experience it for ourselves. Few times in a traditional classroom setting does this kind of opportunity exist.
>
> Our children have learned math, history, geography, and sewing skills through this project, but more importantly, they feel as if they have made a difference in the world, a difference that is real and tangible. They have learned about love and were able to experience and share it.

There were other times when our children demonstrated evidence of translating their learning to action. Students in a number of classes made visits to local personal care and nursing homes during the school year. These visitations were an opportunity for the children to learn the value of being a good neighbor while developing a sense of goodwill toward the sick and elderly of the community. The student government, on its own initiative, suggested, organized, and accomplished a neighborhood cleanup in the spring of the year. On a designated Saturday morning, students, teachers, parents, and I met at the school to clean and beautify the school grounds by raking leaves, pulling weeds, and planting flowers. There were also small groups who picked up trash from sidewalks and other public areas within a two-block radius of the school.

Another activity organized by the student government, again on its own initiative, was a year-end assembly in which each grade level produced a performance of its choosing that depicted one or more of the character-related attributes emphasized throughout the year. These performances were original works and involved almost every classroom in the school. Parents were invited to the full-school assembly to witness the students perform. This was truly a special activity, leaving many with teary eyes and bringing a multitude of positive comments to the faculty and administration about the benefits of the character education program. These and other initiatives occurred as a means of integrating the concepts of responsibility, respect, love, hope, loyalty, honesty, justice, and courage in the total school community. Each activity clearly related to the development of character.

There was also evidence that students were actively using their character learning in the community. There were instances when unsolicited testimony came from community sources. One afternoon, a call came to the school office from a woman who wished to speak to the principal to report an incident involving one of our students. This happened from time to time, usually in the form of a complaint. In this instance, the call was positive. The woman reported that a student from our school had held a door open for her at a local shopping mall. She commented that it had been a long time since she had experienced such an act from a young person. The holding of doors had also increased in school among students and by students for school personnel and guests. In one instance, a guest approaching the school from outside observed a student on the inside notice her approaching and change direction to come to open the door and welcome her to the school.

In another instance, a local clergyman was distributing communion to a number of young first communicants. One group of students voiced a "thank you" when handed the host and others did not. When the clergyman commented about this later, he was told that those children who expressed thanks were students from our school. There were also numerous times when guests in the school came to the principal's office to comment on the exceptional kindness and courtesies extended to them during their visit. In addition, substitute teachers regularly wrote notes and commented to the regular classroom teacher and the principal about the "other than ordinary" experiences of observed and personal interactions with and among the students. Representative examples from substitute teacher forms follow:

Excellent behavior. Students were very helpful during opening exercises. I commended them on their behavior, as well as on their uncommonly good manners toward one another.

I usually prefer substituting for intermediate grades. I must say that I enjoyed your class very much. They listened and they interacted well with one another. They responded well to change. I am impressed. It says a great deal about their teacher and the entire school environment.

These statements from substitute teachers are a sample of numerous unsolicited confirmations that there had been an impact resulting from the influence of the integrated character education initiative.

In general, the results of my dissertation research revealed a positive effect resulting from the implementation of the character education program. Data collected from teachers and parents of students in the school indicated that change had occurred in the students during the year of the study. Teachers reported pleasure in observing an increase in positive, cooperative, and caring attitudes among students and a willingness to learn that had not been experienced in previous years. Teachers commented repeatedly about student enthusiasm and the cooperative manner in which students worked with teachers and peers. Students began to appropriately use the character-related vocabulary in their daily interactions with peers and school personnel. They were able to apply the taught character-related concepts to real-life situations and, in comparison to previous years, there was a significant increase in student displays of respect and in the use of manners and common courtesy among students and between students and school personnel.

To me, as principal of the school, it was dramatically evident that there had been a tremendous improvement in student behavior and overall school climate. This is not only attributable to the consistent delivery of the formal character education curriculum, but equally, or possibly even more importantly, to the integrated approach that enabled us to bridge the gap from learning to action. I believe that a critical factor in the positive impact of any character instruction is the fact that implementation of the curriculum should include an integrated approach in which the concepts of character development are modeled in every aspect of the schools' academic and extracurricular program. I also firmly believe that implementation of a formal character education curriculum alone would not have as positive an impact without an integrated philosophy.

It is known that the introduction of ethics education programs has at times met with strong opposition from community sources due to the concern that schools were infringing on the responsibilities of parents in values education. My study and the implementation of values instruction in our school did not receive a single opposing comment from parents, community, or school officials. Parents overwhelmingly endorsed the character development initiatives and were definitively supportive in expressing their opinion that the program should remain a permanent part of the overall school program.

Our school has become a community of learners where we continue to be successful at teaching the subject matter taught in any traditional elementary school, but our school culture has changed, largely due to the teaching of character. We were successful at bridging the difficult gap from learning to action. What the head knows, the heart can translate to action. Our good school is well on its way to becoming a great school.

REFERENCES

Heartwood Institute. (1993). *Heartwood: An ethics curriculum for children.* (Available from the Heartwood Institute, 465 N. Craig St., Pittsburgh, PA 15213)
Mills, L. A. (1991). *The rag coat.* New York: Little, Brown.
Porter, B. C. (1982). *Miss Rumphius.* New York: Viking.

Principle Three

A Positive School Environment Helps Build Character

5

Building a Positive Classroom Environment

MARK JOHN TIERNO

Campus Executive Officer and Dean
University of Wisconsin, Sheboygan

"Education has for its object the formation of character."
—Herbert Spencer (1850)

Educational and developmental theorists have long held that schooling experiences impart a significant impact on the personality growth of both children and youth. The works of John Dewey (1902, 1915) and Maria Montessori (1912/1964, 1936/1966) as well as more recent contributions—for example those of Erik Erikson (1950, 1950/ 1968, 1959), Thomas Good and Jere Brophy (1991), Robert Havighurst (1968, 1983), Havinghust and Hilda Taba (1949), Kevin Ryan and Thomas Lickona (1987), and Ralph Tyler (1978)—all point to the variety of experiences students gain in school that leave their marks on social-emotional growth and the development of character in personality. Clearly, teachers and their professional colleagues are not always able to ensure that the impact of every classroom experience is constructive and positive. In many ways, the school represents a social environment over which students exercise significant control. Yet, given that most social learning occurs through observation and imitation (Bandura, 1986; Good & Brophy, 1991; Miller & Dollard, 1941), educators do shoulder a special responsibility to make certain that our classrooms represent positive environments in which children are able to grow in beneficial ways. For this reason, teachers need to consider the extent to which their own classroom behaviors—words, deeds, and the consistency between the two—represent undeniably powerful models that can contribute to the positive development of character in their students.

Given the importance of schooling experiences in the formation of those qualities of personality associated with an individual's character—especially values, ethics, and morals—many educators and informed observers of educational processes stress the need for schools to address more explicitly the formation of values, ethics, and morals in students and in so doing to participate actively in helping to form the character of those students (Havighurst, 1983; Kohlberg & Turiel, 1971; Purkey, 1970; Ryan & Lickona, 1987; Tierno, 1983). Many of these experts focus their recommendations on ways to incorporate moral development in the curriculum. The contents of the humanities, the social sciences, and the natural sciences are replete with questions that relate directly to values, ethics, and morals. Yet, given the emphasis placed on the importance of social interaction, observation, and imitation in the process of personal growth, it would appear shortsighted to argue that the contents of the curriculum exercise the most important influence in the classroom. Rather, it is the teacher's own behaviors that appear to be the singularly most significant variable in determining the extent to which a classroom environment positively contributes to the social growth of students.

CHARACTER REFLECTED IN TEACHER BEHAVIORS

Besides rendering curricular decisions, educators also face another set of challenges in relation to the way they contribute to the growth and development of character in their students. As representatives of the wider adult society, teachers should always represent models of moral and ethical adult behavior. It is not at all new to point out that teachers serve as role models for their students. Yet, despite the apparently widespread recognition that they do represent models for their students, few teachers receive any training that helps them to consider the manner in which their status as role models should guide their exchanges with students or the behaviors they exhibit to students. Many teachers regularly make statements and exhibit behaviors in the classroom that represent the antithesis of those that would be described as appropriate models. This is true in three crucial and related areas: the ways in which teachers interact with their students and with others in view of their students, the ways they go about instructing their students, and the ways they manage off-task and uncooperative students.

A teacher exhibiting a behavior, or engaging in an act, in the view of one or more students is, in effect, providing a model for students to emulate. The mere fact that the teacher engages in the action suggests to students that they may choose that behavior for themselves. Since most social learning results from observation and imitation, teachers need to consider carefully every aspect of their conduct—no matter how seemingly minor—that students can observe. As they go about their many tasks in the classroom, then, teachers need to recognize and respond to the power inherent in their status as role models.

When they engage students in learning experiences and when they direct and redirect student activities and behaviors, teachers should strive to achieve three major objectives in terms of their own conduct.

First, teachers need to model appropriate interactions for their students. Teachers interact with their students for a wide variety of reasons in the classroom prior to, during, and following instruction; between classes; in other locations in the school, such as the cafeteria or the hallways; at school-sponsored performance, social, and athletic events; and in other settings away from the school. Each of these interactions has the potential to impart an impact of many different kinds and qualities. In both conscious and unconscious ways, students see each and every teacher behavior as a potential behavior that they may adopt for themselves. This appears to be particularly true of those behaviors exhibited by teachers for whom students feel sincere respect.

Second, each teacher needs to develop an instructional approach or style that serves as a model of learning for students. It should represent a model that reflects the fact that the teacher is a learner, one who enjoys the challenges and ambiguities inherent in the learning process. Rather than attempting to present themselves as fonts of information who are capable of answering virtually any question without error, teachers should be seen by their students as individuals who enjoy the various activities associated with learning. These positive role-modeling teachers demonstrate to students that they can "figure things out" for themselves and, equally, enjoy cooperating with others in the process of thinking and learning. Teachers should model the processes through which both they and their students can define questions or problems for study, generate hypotheses or alternate explanations, use curricular materials as pieces of evidence to answer questions or resolve problems, and state answers or conclusions based on their understanding of the evidence gathered and examined. As teachers display these inquisitive qualities, they also exemplify the message that learning is most often a cooperative meaning-making process, not a memorizing act. An effective teaching style encourages students to view their teacher as a partner in the learning process (Lickona, 1987). In all of this, teachers should always be supportive when students experience difficulties, appreciative of student propositions, and respectful of student efforts.

Third, teachers need to devise approaches to classroom management that motivate students to stay on task and to cooperate both with the teacher and with each other. Simultaneously, the ways teachers manage students should serve as models of the very kinds of cooperative and respectful interpersonal relationships already described. Management strategies and techniques that rely on verbal intimidation, biting sarcasm, oppressive forms of punishment, or physical intimidation may temporarily achieve results in student compliance with teacher directives. Yet, educators who regularly model these negative forms of conduct confirm to students that these very behaviors represent acceptable forms of interpersonal interaction. Clearly, displaying these negative behaviors sends the wrong message to students. Recognizing this fact places a major challenge before teachers. They must devise management plans that extend their modeling of interactions and learning behaviors to their approaches to managing even the most challenging of students. Those educators who care about the influence they exert on students' character formation need to consider carefully the ways they choose to interact with all students, including those students whose actions reflect a lack of interest, cooperation, or respect. To do otherwise sends the erroneous message that principled human interaction may be limited to those situations in which people agree with each other. Teachers must model exactly the opposite—that respect for individuals or groups remains a valued goal even in situations that involve disagreement, no matter how strongly held.

MODELING INTERACTIONS

Teachers who employ an autocratic style, although apparently viewed as successful by some observers, are not modeling the kinds of behaviors that are expected and rewarded in the wider society. Such teachers appear to perceive their students as underlings to be ordered about rather than as fellow travelers in a quest for understanding. To a great extent, the perceptions that teachers and students hold about each other represent primary causes of difficulties in the ways they communicate with each other.

> The teacher as teacher does not accept the student as a total person nor does the student accept the teacher as such. The teacher accepts the student insofar as he [or she] is a person. The teacher . . . is a task-master with objective standards that devastate any personal acceptance based upon mutual regard and affection alone. (Cervantes, 1965, p. 113)

Cervantes's observation can be useful to those teachers who recognize the need to improve the quality of their relationships with their students to properly recognize the extent to which students learn from the ways teachers go about their business of teaching. Galbo (1989) strongly suggests that the quality of the relationship between teachers and students should take on primary importance, representing an end in itself rather than a means to other ends.

To establish and maintain positive classroom environments, teachers should always endeavor to serve as models of appropriate behavior. Effective classroom teachers recognize that every time they say or do anything, the way they state words and engage in deeds—no matter how apparently inconsequential—communicates messages of their own, including the message that each such behavior is one that students may choose to adopt. For these reasons, teachers ought to make efforts to establish respectful and trusting relationships with their students (Galbo, 1983, 1984; George et al., 1992; Tierno, 1991). Earning the respect and trust of students may require effort, especially when some students have had the benefit of too few, if any, experiences with teachers in whom they have been able to place their genuine trust. In fact, as children grow, an "us versus them" mentality develops in their relationships with teachers. Teachers who do not model behaviors that reflect a respect for students fail as role models for them.

Students prefer teachers who appear to understand them and show an interest in them as people, both as a group and as individuals (Chase, 1981). As students grow, they react well to teachers who demonstrate their respect for students by treating them in ways that reflect a recognition of their maturing capacities (Galbo, 1983, 1984). Another way to understand students' desire for relationships based on respect, trust, interest, and understanding is to say that students respond best to teachers whose interactions communicate a fundamental confidence in their students. In their varied relationships with students, those teachers who successfully establish respectful relationships with their students achieve both the greatest success in the teaching of subject matter and the most positive impact as exemplars, or role models. Galbo (1989) puts it well when he states that most students "prefer the same characteristics and qualities in their relationships with adults that adults prefer with each other" (p. 554).

Teachers represent powerful role models. For this reason, in all their interactions with students they should always strive to be polite and well mannered. They should make certain to say "please" when asking for student compliance and "thank you" in response to both cooperation and effort. Teachers should make every effort to treat their students with respect, expect to receive respect from their students, and expect students to behave respectfully toward each other. In these ways, teachers both model the behaviors they expect of students and establish a learning environment that is supportive and humane.

TEACHERS AS MODEL LEARNERS

Although many observers of education debate about the relative successes and failures of contemporary schools, few critics argue about the importance of teachers and the significance of their impact on student development. Yet, too much of the attention directed toward teaching and learning concentrates on questions related to issues that are undeniably narrow, such as improving standardized test score results. This concern has been the focus of federal educational policies since the publication of *A Nation at Risk* by the National Commission on Excellence in Education (1983). Interestingly, when other, more knowledgeable critics add their voices to the debate, they typically concentrate on the extent to which academic achievement can be improved by a change in curricular focus or methodological approach rather than advocating a more fundamental change in the goals schools pursue.

Two major reviews of contemporary schools that are often positively characterized as informed alternatives to the positions offered in *A Nation at Risk*—those authored by Ernest Boyer (1983) and John Goodlad (1984)—represent examples of critiques that recognize the need for students to experience both greater breadth in the content of the curriculum and increased opportunities to engage in learning that fosters problem-solving capacities. Yet, significantly, both Goodlad and Boyer fail to direct sufficient attention toward issues related to the impact of the classroom environment on the formation of character in students. The ways teachers choose to go about the business of teaching do more than influence standardized test scores. Teaching style influences the extent to which students feel competent about themselves as learners (Purkey, 1970; Tierno, 1983). Just as important, however, may be the impact teaching style has on the ways students perceive the learning act. One of the most essential repercussions of instructional style is that it directly influences the character of students as students, as learners, and as thinkers. The act of teaching should serve as a model for students, a model that exemplifies the attitudes, skills, and behaviors needed for effectiveness as a thinking, learning adult.

One study of 2,670 students and 137 teachers in four different school systems found that teachers who were viewed as superior "model the pursuit of knowledge. They show excitement and curiosity about knowledge, feel personal payoff in problem-solving, demonstrate that answers are not fixed and new skills and insights are necessary and useful, encourage observation and analysis and are committed to the success and involvement of their students" (Olsen & Moore, 1984, p. 19).

In the classroom, virtually every action a teacher undertakes during the process of instruction should, among other things, serve as a model for students, modeling an interest in making sense out of that which is unclear, in making personal meaning out of that which may at first seem either confusing or remote or both (Good & Brophy, 1991). Most important, the transmission of our most cherished cultural traditions and the mobilization of students to action should not only come from discussions about character and culture, it also should be motivated by the ways in which teachers engage students in such discus-

sions. The teacher whose instructional style recognizes that constructive character development is fostered successfully when the curriculum incorporates opportunities for meaningful discussions about culture and character simultaneously models the very characteristics the
curriculum supports.

Directly related to the modeling of behaviors based on cherished
cultural concepts, such as justice and equality, during the instructional
process is the need to do so when students get off task or when they
behave unappreciatively. It may be relatively easy to demonstrate respect toward and trust in students who are cooperative, but it is equally
important to maintain consistency in this regard when students, for
whatever reasons, choose not to cooperate. From the perspective of
teacher-as-model, it is in the realm of classroom management that
many teachers find it most difficult to display behaviors that serve as
models for their students.

MODELING FOR CLASSROOM MANAGEMENT

Among the many decisions educators need to consider carefully in relation to the building of positive classroom environments, those about
classroom management deserve especially thorough consideration.
Even when teachers make every effort to design interesting learning
activities, instances still occur when problem behaviors necessitate
management interventions (Tierno, 1991). In fact, it may be that decisions about why, when, and how to redirect off-task students are
among the most troublesome decisions teachers regularly face. This is
unquestionably true for those teachers who express concerns about the
values reflected in the ways they decide to manage their classrooms.
These teachers find that some commonly used management techniques
tend to be ineffective and others may actually serve to increase the
number of disruptions in their classes.

Some teachers use autocratic management approaches that confront their students person to person in the presence of peers. Most students are embarrassed and upset by such confrontations, even when
they respond by complying with the teacher's directives. These students may harbor anger, fear, or other negative feelings about their
teacher as a direct result of such embarrassments, feelings that could
create problems during future interactions and that may reduce the

teacher's effectiveness. When confronted by their teacher in the presence of peers, some off-task students may feel compelled to defend themselves either by denying any wrongdoing or by issuing verbal rebukes of their own. Other students may strike back verbally. Whatever the student's motivation, many teachers then feel their authority in the classroom will be undermined unless the student who answers back receives a public response. A verbal tug of war often results in such situations. When this happens, a teacher actually surrenders authority by engaging in debate as the student's equal. Even worse, the forms of teacher conduct described in this scenario are antithetical to those that would represent models for students.

Engaging in public debates with off-task students is clearly undesirable because it undermines both the teacher's authority in the classroom and the trust and respect teachers should be seeking to develop with their students. Furthermore, the use of confrontation as a management technique suggests to students that such person-to-person confrontations represent appropriate behaviors in their own interpersonal relationships. To model appropriate behavior in the ways they go about interacting with students, teachers should avoid needless confrontations by employing "task-focused" approaches to classroom management—that is, they should use management techniques that focus on the tasks at hand, not on the behaviors of particular individuals.

Exclamations such as "Stop talking, Jimmy!" or "Get back to your seat, Maria!" represent relatively minor examples of an unnecessarily autocratic classroom style and, for this reason alone, do not appear desirable. Statements such as these also serve as examples of "approval-focused" rather than task-focused statements. These teacher-initiated confrontations communicate the teacher's personal disapproval and also suggest how the student should respond to receive approval. In most instances, students do comply. Yet, despite the likelihood of student compliance, statements of this kind do not represent examples of model interactions. Also, given their desire for social acceptance, many students abhor being singled out and ridiculed in public. For this reason, they rarely trust and respect teachers who regularly confront them, even when their own behaviors warrant redirection by their teacher. Some students resist or even defy their teachers when confronted with teacher disapproval while in the company of their classmates.

Instead of confronting students in public, teachers should find ways to redirect off-task behavior with words and deeds that show respect for students as individuals and therefore model the kinds of respectful interactions our society expects of adults. For all these reasons, the use of task-focused management approaches seems especially prudent. Reinforcing statements such as "I like the way you managed that assignment" or "I can see that you're really good at this!" support the learner, model positive behavior, decrease the likelihood of confrontation, and foster a larger sense of competence and self-worth in the student.

TEACHERS' MODELING BUILDS A POSITIVE CLASSROOM ENVIRONMENT

Many educational theorists recognize the need for educators to influence the formation of values, ethics, and morals in students and to do so in constructive and positive classroom environments. Classroom teachers are directly involved in helping to form the character of their students and doing so in positive ways. Many educators recognize the need to incorporate learning experiences that promote character development in the curriculum. Indeed, the humanities, the social sciences, and the natural sciences are replete with issues that relate directly to values, ethics, and morals. But given the emphasis placed on social interaction, observation, and imitation in social learning in general and character formation in particular, it would appear erroneous to argue that the most important influence exerted on students is exercised by the contents of the curriculum alone.

Respectful interaction, effective instruction, and successful management of students all require careful attention and planning. Most important, as teachers consider and decide how to interact, instruct, and manage, they need to remember that their own words and actions represent powerful models in the classroom. Teachers serve as role models. Effective and respected teachers represent especially powerful role models. For this reason, they must appear polite and well mannered. They should make every effort to treat their students with respect if they expect to receive respect from the students and if they expect students to respect each other. By modeling behaviors that are consistent with our democratic culture's most cherished values—including responsibility, participation, diversity, and privacy as well as justice and equality—teachers interested in building a positive classroom environment that encourages learning while also positively influencing student character development will be able to do both through the content of the curriculum and through the way they implement the curriculum.

REFERENCES

Bandura, A. (1986). *Social foundations of thought and action: A social cognitive theory.* Englewood Cliffs, NJ: Prentice Hall.

Boyer, E. L. (1983). *High school: A report on secondary education in America.* New York: Harper & Row.

Cervantes, L. F. (1965). *The dropout: Causes and cures.* Ann Arbor: University of Michigan Press.

Chase, C. I. (1981). Teenagers are mostly positive about high school. *Phi Delta Kappan, 62,* 526.

Dewey, J. (1902). *The child and the curriculum.* Chicago: University of Chicago Press.

Dewey, J. (1915). *The school and society* (rev. ed.). Chicago: University of Chicago Press.

Erikson, E. H. (1950). *Childhood and society.* New York: Norton.

Erikson, E. H. (1959). Identity and the life cycle: Selected papers. *Psychological Issues Monograph Series 1: No. 1.* New York: International Universities Press.

Erikson, E. H. (1968). *Identity: Youth and crisis.* New York: Norton. (Original work published 1950)

Galbo, J. J. (1983). Adolescents' perceptions of significant adults: A review of literature. *Adolescence, 18,* 417-427.

Galbo, J. J. (1984). Adolescents' perceptions of significant adults: A review of literature. *Adolescence, 19,* 951-968.

Galbo, J. J. (1989). The teacher as significant adult: A review of literature. *Adolescence, 24,* 549-555.

George, P. S., et al. (1992). *The middle school—and beyond.* Alexandria, VA: Association for Supervision and Curriculum Development.

Good, T. L., & Brophy, J. E. (1991). *Looking in classrooms* (5th ed.) New York: HarperCollins.

Goodlad, J. I. (1984). *A place called school: Prospects for the future.* New York: McGraw-Hill.

Havighurst, R. J. (1968). The middle school child in contemporary society. *Theory Into Practice, 7,* 120-122.

Havighurst, R. J. (1983). *Developmental tasks and education* (4th ed.). New York: David McKay.

Havighurst, R. J., & Taba, H. (1949). *Adolescent character and personality.* New York: Chapman & Hall.

Kohlberg, L., & Turiel, E. (1971). Moral development and moral education. In G. Lesser (Ed.), *Psychology and educational practice.* Chicago: Scott, Foresman.

Lickona, T. (1987). Character development in the elementary school. In K. Ryan & G. McLean (Eds.), *Character development in schools and beyond* (pp. 177-205). New York: Praeger.

Miller, N. E., & Dollard, M. J. (1941). *Social learning and imitation.* New Haven, CT: Yale University Press.

Montessori, M. (1964). *The Montessori method* (A. E. George, Trans.). New York: Schocken. (Original work published 1912)

Montessori, M. (1966). *The secret of childhood* (M. J. Costelloe, Trans.). Notre Dame, IN: Fides. (Original work published 1936)

National Commission on Excellence in Education. (1983). *A nation at risk: The imperative for educational reform.* Washington, DC: Government Printing Office.

Olsen, L., & Moore, M. (1984). *Voices from the classroom: Students and teachers speak out on the quality of teaching in our schools.* Oakland, CA: Citizens Policy Center. (ERIC Document Reproduction Service No. ED 252 497)

Purkey, W. W. (1970). *Self concept and school achievement.* Englewood Cliffs, NJ: Prentice Hall.

Ryan, K., & Lickona, T. (1987). Character development: The challenge and the model. In K. Ryan & G. F. McLean (Eds.), *Character development in schools and beyond.* New York: Praeger.

Tierno, M. J. (1983). Responding to self concept disturbance among early adolescents: A psychosocial view for educators. *Adolescence, 18,* 577-584.

Tierno, M. J. (1991). Responding to the socially motivated behaviors of early adolescents: Recommendations for classroom management. *Adolescence, 26,* 569-577.

Tyler, R. (1978). *From youth to constructive adult life: The role of the public school.* San Francisco: McCutchan.

6

More Than a
Good Lesson Plan

KENNETH BARBOUR

Principal, Tenth Street School
Oakmont, Pennsylvania

"The end of learning is the formation of character."
—Kiabara Ekken (1710)

For almost three decades, I have witnessed how the power of a school environment that focuses on character development can shape the attitudes and lives of children. For 10 years of my professional life, I worked as a classroom teacher, for 15 years as a building principal, and for 2 years I have been the superintendent of the Wilkinsburg School District, which borders the city of Pittsburgh. One of the most rewarding aspects of my career is that all of this work has been done in inner-city schools. These are the schools that are almost always associated with violence, apathy, defiance, and poor academic achievement. Yet, I know I have made a difference, because I have used character education as a vehicle to motivate and inspire children and teachers.

For years, I have been used as a consultant and lecturer on the issue of character education to numerous area schools. Many schools in the Pittsburgh region have asked me to speak to parent groups, teachers, and students about the impact school environments have on the promotion of character in our youth. For me, character education is one of the fundamental issues we must address if we are to make any kind of serious and long-term impact on the social and academic destiny of our children.

CHARACTER EDUCATION DEFINED

To me, character education is the development of a language with students that instills in them universal values that are worldwide (Rusnak, Burrett, & Farrelly, 1993). These basic human values include such concepts as honesty, trust, cooperation, respect, responsibility, hope, determination, and loyalty. These are important and accepted qualities that all parents would want for their children. They are values all of us need regardless of our race, religion, economic status, or any other defining characteristics to promote a healthy, livable, and workable society. Yet, in many urban districts, families have failed in their effort to give the children the guidance they need to develop these important qualities. Therefore, the school must fill the void.

From a very pragmatic view, these character qualities are profoundly important to develop in young people. These qualities are often the essence of what employers look for when they hire or evaluate performance on the job. Employers want employees who are honest, dependable, responsible, punctual, and trustworthy. By teaching these qualities in our schools, we are giving young people a formula for future success. By ignoring these issues we not only fail our students, but we also fail our responsibility to society to help craft contributing citizens.

I believe we can be successful; we can promote academic success and ensure a productive future for our children by developing learning environments that promote character. I have seen it succeed.

THE MANCHESTER PROGRAM

My first administrative assignment was as principal of Manchester Elementary School, one of the largest elementary schools in the city of Pittsburgh school system. This school is located in one of the oldest parts of Pittsburgh and has a 99% minority student population drawn from families with low socioeconomic status and income levels. The problems at the school and around the community were exacerbated by escalating violence, gangs, drugs, and crime. Moreover, it seemed that as the community problems grew, the academic achievement and social attitudes of students declined.

One of my first actions as the new principal of Manchester Elementary School was to implement a school environment that emphasized character. It was obvious to me that the standard formula of filling children with math and reading skills did little to promote the very behaviors they needed to succeed in those subjects. As a faculty, we began to discuss and plan lessons around concepts such as hope, respect, cooperation, and all the other basic human values that foster good citizenship. We established value-oriented themes that tied together social studies, music, and art and generally promoted the notion of "good citizenship" throughout the school. Most important, we created an environment of respect, responsibility, and cooperation.

Teachers promoted these concepts in their classrooms through lessons and *modeling behavior.* I watched, sometimes in amazement, as many of our students grew into responsible members of our school community. Children began to accept more responsibility for their actions, and the school became more manageable. There was a substantial increase in student achievement and this had a multiplying effect as it increased the self-esteem of the students. I also witnessed a dramatic decrease in the number of suspensions, office referrals, and student absences.

Of equal importance, I also noticed a positive change in the attitudes of the professional staff. As teachers witnessed the improved atmosphere at the school, their self-confidence improved. They began to believe that they were making a difference in the lives of the children because this new approach to working in our school was producing positive results. A new energy was also transmitted by teachers to students and the overall environment of the school changed from one of pessimism to one of hope and confidence. We knew that something very good and special was happening in this often-forgotten school in the corner of the city. Optimism and self-esteem became part of the school culture as our efforts to develop character began to take shape.

Tricia Sutton, a science specialist at Manchester, related her experiences with character education:

> We began focusing on character development in our school to give the students a blueprint for success. By modeling a community that fostered cooperation and discussion of academic and social problems children began to "work through" their own personal problems and this promoted a supportive school environment. Understanding how and why the circumstance or problem had occurred gave the children something tangible with which to work. For example, if a child was called a name by another child, before he called something back at the offending child, he learned to think about the values and action that could spread into a violent confrontation. This is not an easy task for anyone, much less children who witness on an almost daily basis that blind retaliation is an acceptable pathway to solving disputes. However, children were shown a systematic alternative that modeled another way of handling situations instead of physical actions to end disputes.

Another successful tactic we used at Manchester Elementary School was a whole-class discussion model. By generating class discussions based on a different value each month, the children became familiar with the vocabulary of values as well as actions or options to be taken to accept responsibilities. Concepts such as kindness, courtesy, honesty, respect, commitment, and courage were defined and discussed. Of course, teachers made every effort to model these concepts through their own behaviors. Teachers and students would talk about school and neighborhood *incidents* and suggest alternative strategies as to how to *deal with* a range of problems that confront these children in their daily lives both in and out of school.

One thing we discovered very early in our discussions with children was that their understanding of the concepts that surround character was often dramatically different from that of adults. Many of the children, for example, thought that courage was something only associated with battle and confrontation. Many children saw courage as the "mark" of an adult, as they often witnessed older children and adults bully others and engage in street fights or other acts of violence. Other children saw courage as defiance of any type of authority, no matter how reasonable. As one teacher discussed the concept of courage, a child asked, "Do you mean I'm showing courage when I walk away from a fight?" The discussion continued and was reaffirmed by teachers and other students. The student was incredulous. It was a major paradigm shift for that child to realize that one could be courageous when one did *not* fight, confront, or defy.

The experience of this discussion was shared by teachers at our weekly planning meeting. It was one of those very emotional, even profound, times in teachers' careers when we knew we made a difference. That incident and others like it confirmed our suspicion that the environment we were developing in our school was already paying dividends. We were well on our way to building a strong school!

WEST SIDE ACADEMY

My second experience as an administrator came when I was assigned to reopen a school that had been closed for a number of years. The building was located in an area that according to police statistics had the highest crime rate of any area in Pittsburgh. The school was reopened amid a storm of protests from community representatives, state and local officials, parents, and other concerned people.

The protests stemmed from a concern for the physical safety of the children. The neighborhood around West Side Academy consisted almost entirely of public housing projects. Drug dealers, gang wars, crimes, and drive-by shootings were commonplace. Many community members gave little chance for the school's survival, with dire predictions that children would be harmed.

Originally, 155 students in Grades K-5 and seven staff members were assigned to the school. Some of the students came from intact families, but some came from unstable homes and for them the school had to take on a parental role. I realized that my first project was to work with the teachers to establish an environment that promoted character growth in the children.

One of the first things we did to enhance the school environment was to display schoolwide themes focused on values and character development. Hallway banners were fashioned to announce our intent and classrooms were decorated with signs and slogans that strongly encouraged such valued human traits as honesty, courage, cooperation, respect, and responsibility.

As a beginning tool, I introduced the teachers to concepts and practices that addressed character development. Many of these tactics were adapted from the Thomas Jefferson Center for Character Education of Los Angeles, California, and refined in my former assignment at Manchester Elementary School. This approach focused on a strong school environment where teachers modeled and discussed issues such as hope, respect, responsibility, cooperation, and honesty. Teachers also decorated the school with signs and banners that clearly announced that our school was united in its determination to foster character growth. From this blueprint, the teachers began to contribute their own ideas to slowly weave the teaching of character into the academic and social life of the school.

One schoolwide activity included an honor roll for students who demonstrated good character. All students competed to be recognized on this laminated clipboard that listed the names of students who exemplified good character traits for that month. The names were written with overhead marker and changed monthly. This simple approach helped focus the students and staff on the issue of character development in our school and became a centerpiece for discussion and reflection by students and staff. The honor roll concept carried over to the individual classrooms. Lessons and rules were developed to enhance a class's or individual's opportunity to be listed in the honor roll. The concept of character development became infectious as all academic classes as well as art, music, reading, and physical education began infusing the notion of character education in their classes.

Gail Friedman, a fifth-grade teacher, explained how character education was addressed in her class at West Side Academy:

> My class addressed a character theme each month and added ways in which we could meet the goals of each character trait. This led to lessons on critical thinking skills and setting goals. . . . The students' ideas were all placed on poster paper, discussed, hung in the hallway and read as part of our opening exercises. Throughout the month, we reminded each other of the theme and congratulated each other too. The teachers stressed and wanted the students to

understand that there is a path to success, and everyone can achieve it through cooperation and good character.

Other teachers used the focus on character education in writing assignments. Students began keeping and maintaining writing journals to document their good deed for the day and teachers supplemented these experiences with assignments such as, "Describe the day you felt like a star in your classroom or in the eyes of your parents."

Positive comments and statements were recognized and rewarded on bulletin boards and in announcements. Teachers, for example, took it on themselves to eliminate the use of the term "Shut up!" from the school. After they modeled alternatives for this term and highlighted it to the students, many visitors noticed the reduction of disrespectful speech in the school.

To stress the power our comments have on others, the teachers instructed each student to stand and speak while facing the audience (class). In this way, only thought-filled opinions and answers were given because all eyes were on *you*. It cut down on off-task comments that often produce snickers among students.

We also felt that the first day of school was the most important. This is the time when students are most impressionable and we were sure that if we acted with a good amount of consistency that the whole concept of being a better person would be infectious and last throughout the year.

Our first-day assembly emphasized the values we would focus on all year. The words respect, responsibility, trust, cooperation, and hope were all but chanted as teachers talked about what their expectations were of each student and what each student could expect of every teacher.

For the next several school days, a frequent discussion that teachers had with their classes evolved around the positive character traits that we highlighted in our school and how we may apply them to others. One teacher told the story to her students of how her former class went to an overnight camp that was staffed by student volunteers from a local college. One camp counselor, expecting the worst from our children, shouted out "O.K. Now . . . Shut up!" A stunned silence came over the group, but much to the amazement of the counselor it was not a silence of obedience to the order. After a few seconds of awkward quiet, the students together walked up to the young man and politely said, "Excuse me! We don't talk like that to each other!" This simple story demonstrated to the children that our students could make a difference in people's attitudes. It showed them the positive power of character education.

During my years at West Side Academy, I developed the habit of collecting comments about the school from students and parents. One parent wrote me a note as I resigned my principalship. It read, in part, "Children should learn about character, so that they can grow up as responsible, honest and trustworthy persons." A student wrote, "This school reminds us that we need to be honest and trustworthy to everyone around us." Finally, in reflecting on his school experience, one young man said, "This has helped me by constantly reminding me to think about what I'm doing to others and cooperate, because if I didn't I would be in serious trouble."

The teachers at West Side Academy continue the legacy of character development in the school. Gail Friedman, a fifth-grade teacher, describes integrating character in the daily routine of the schools as easy to manage, quick, and effective: "The schoolwide implementation enables students and teachers to share the same vocabulary." Other teachers note splendid results both socially and academically.

Today, West Side Academy continues to do a splendid job with children. Parents have become involved and recently insisted on a dress code for students. Test scores have steadily improved, and poor discipline is not a dominant factor in the school. Character education is still alive and well at West Side—this in a school that the community did not want to reopen! It is now a school with a waiting list of hopeful families trying to get the best and safest education for their children.

RESERVE ELEMENTARY SCHOOL

As news of our success at both Manchester and West Side Academy spread, other teachers in school districts throughout the region began working on character education approaches. One school was the Reserve Elementary School in an adjoining suburban school district. Kristen Hoffman, a music teacher in the school, began using children's literature to demonstrate the power of character. She used stories that exemplified basic human values. Then, through projects and discussions that centered on a variety of cultures, children began to understand the ways people are similar in their approach to values. Hoffman notes, "As a music teacher at Reserve Elementary School, I serve mostly as a resource person. When the individual classes are assigned a topic to present to the entire school, I locate and teach appropriate songs. I also make cassette tapes for practice in the classrooms and accompany the students on the piano during assemblies." This supplemental approach enhances the learning environment and shows children that the building of a good person is not only for a homeroom teacher.

Other comments came from Nadene Hinds, an art teacher at Reserve School:

> As an art teacher, I am basically used as a resource person for our school projects. I have always enjoyed integrating art with other subjects, and the benefits to the students are immeasurable. I assist the teachers with sculptures, murals, banners, scenery, costumes, and jewelry that follow the theme. These creative projects when combined with character development enhance the students' understanding, confidence, and esteem.

These successful teachers attest to the fact that character education is best addressed in a total school environment. It is not something that should be confined to a classroom or subject. It is part of the school experience, and teachers of art, music, and physical education can certainly contribute to the development of character.

CHARACTER IN OUR SCHOOLS

For years, teachers have been teaching values in their classrooms, but today educators are finding it imperative to build values into the environment of the school.

The cornerstone of the school environment is the development of an integrated approach to character education, one that energizes the organization of the school and the environment around basic human values. Through this approach, I have found that children monitor their own actions and begin to problem-solve and resolve conflicts.

Students in a learning environment that fosters character growth through discussion and action learn how to accept consequences for their actions and develop and improve their self-confidence, self-esteem, and positive attitudes. They are then able to set and achieve realistic goals. The curricula are easy to implement, to use, and to infuse in the regular curriculum and environment of the school. Character education is something that is not well taught in isolation. Instead, a thematic approach teaches universal values that include honesty, respect, responsibility, commitment, and service to others.

Integrating character in the environment of the school is one of the most important things we can do for our children. My experience has been that when we foster character growth in schools we enhance academics and begin to build a productive person. Some of my findings about including character education in the school follow:

- The development of unified themes that focus on character and values throughout the building promote a positive school environment
- The unifying themes foster cooperative strategies and teaming throughout the school
- A peer tutoring program that is a by-product of a cooperation theme in the school
- Improved academic scores
- Declining behavior problems and, as one teacher noted, "A stronger sense of kindness and generosity demonstrated by our children"

Although several approaches may be used, the most important consideration in developing an environment that promotes character education is the creation of a sense of a positive community with teachers and students. Thematic units that address basic human values may go a long way in promoting discussion and reflection among students. But the power of character education, in my view, lies in the crafting of school and classroom environments that also emphasize modeling, discussion, participation, and hope to students.

Character education is not a remedy for all that ails our schools, but it does give us a blueprint for academic and social success. I have built and witnessed these events in my career and know that character education is more than a good lesson plan.

REFERENCES

Ekken, K. (1710). *The ten precepts.*

Rusnak, T., Burrett, K., & Farrelly, T. (1993). The integrated approach to character education. In T. Lickona & K. Ryan (Eds.), *Character education in schools and beyond.* Washington, DC: Council for Research in Values and Philosophy.

Principle Four

Character Development Is Encouraged Through Administrative Policy and Practice

7

Leadership, Character Growth, and Authenticity

JAMES E. HENDERSON

Dean, School of Education
Duquesne University

*"Are there not some qualities of which all the citizens must
be partakers if there is to be a city at all?"*
—Plato, *The Republic*

To embrace a value system that seeks the good of others before self,
to behave in concert with one's expressed beliefs, and to continually act purposefully and effectively in service of that value system are
the central tenets to the interplay among ethics, leadership, and authenticity. In this chapter, I explore those interrelated concepts, giving attention to the notions of leadership, especially authentic leadership in the
context of the integrated approach to character development. Ethics
and character education and development are treated extensively
throughout this book and are not the sole areas of focus in this chapter.
Moreover, this discussion is rooted in a review of recent leadership lit-

erature as well as an exploration of classic studies in administration and the social sciences.

The educational leader's inclination and ability to develop and maintain organizational systems and policies that line up with the imperatives of ethical and authentic behavior not only define the character of the leader but also the character of the organization itself and the quality of the interactions among organizational constituents. Simply put, if I am a leader, and I "practice what I teach," then I have integrated beliefs and actions. I also then serve as a model for the actions of others in the organization and have defined the standards against which their behavior—and my future behavior—is judged. On the other hand, if I espouse ethical and other-serving behavior but behave in a deceitful, selfish way, I am a hypocrite.

What does it mean, though, for leaders to behave in an authentic fashion? How are the concepts of character growth and authentic leadership interwoven? How does the concept of leader authenticity relate to ethical *and* effective leadership practices in schools? What implications does the relationship among ethics, leadership, and authenticity have for school administrators, teachers, and children?

LEADER AUTHENTICITY

To be authentic, to be genuine, to be real, and to be credible are clearly great virtues in our society and, some would suggest, are the bases of good character. Respect is accorded to those who are observed to behave in an authentic fashion. Inauthentically behaving persons are viewed with distrust and disdain. Authenticity is a cultural precept, derived from ancient traditions of chivalry and respect for admired foes, such that even if one disagrees with another person, one holds that foe in esteem if the foe's actions and expressions appear authentic. An authentic person is viewed as possessing character. Conversely, if one is perceived as behaving in an inauthentic fashion, severe limitations emerge to hinder one's interpersonal ability to function effectively. Although some may view the inauthentic person as having worthy traits and talents, that apprehension seems to be nullified by the misgiving engendered by the perception of inauthenticity, unethical behavior, and questionable character. The implication of that relationship is important for leaders of organizations. Whether the leader is always agreed with, or even liked, by followers is not the issue here. Rather, it appears that the extent to which the leader's followers view the leader as expressing and behaving in an authentic fashion affects the interpersonal effectiveness of the leader and influences the climate of the organization itself.

STUDIES IN ADMINISTRATION

In studies of the organizational climates of schools, Halpin (1966) came to realize that the concept of authenticity, however fuzzy, provided interesting insights and explanations regarding the management of schools. Halpin was struck by the disparity between two types of schools in his study. He observed that in the open schools, the characters (principals and teachers) seemed purposeful in their behavior. In other schools—the closed schools—teachers and administrators seemed to act in a two-dimensional fashion. That is, the people who populated the closed-climate schools did not act for real—they seemed merely to be playing out a part in a less-than-real-life drama. In the open schools, the professional roles of the teachers and the administrators appeared to be subordinate to what the people filling those roles actually were. The teachers and administrators were able to step outside and beyond their role requirements as the situation dictated and were able to maintain an obvious sense of self. In the closed schools, teachers and administrators had their primary sense and source of identification in their role. This salience of role tended to make participants in the school regard their function ritualistically and keep the participants at arm's length, thereby lessening the possibilities for authentic interpersonal relationships.

In discriminating between those who would be authentic and those who would be inauthentic, Halpin (1966) suggested that the principal who was intent on task accomplishment without losing sight of the necessity of being considerate to staff members seemed to be the more authentic individual. This definition and this principal description was reminiscent of the "great person" leader as described by Bales (1958), Carter (1954), and Getzels and Guba (1957) as a transactional leader and later by Burns (1978) and others as a transformational leader, one who would not simply transact business with followers but who would empower them in a true ethical fashion. In fact, an entire issue of *Educational Leadership* was devoted to this topic (Brandt, 1992). In these formulations, the leader was able to move the organization toward task accomplishment and at the same time attend to the social needs of his or her followers. The ability to solve tasks and accomplish goals while providing support for individuals in the organization was seen as a highly desirable, although extremely rare, quality. Halpin indicated that this kind of principal could stand for something and was open in letting the teachers and other school staff know what the school's mission was. In short, the authentic principal exhibited strength of character.

Halpin (1966) also contrasted the open principal's behavior with the behavior of the principal in the closed-climate school. The closed principal did not move the organization to goal accomplishment and typically was not concerned with the need for social support of the school's teachers. The closed principal tended to resist change, to remain aloof from his or her followers, and to ritualize the practices of the organization. The closed principal's behavior showed itself to be two-dimensional and resistant to change. This created the impression with the teaching staff that the principal was not authentic, not to be trusted, and not capable of having authentic interactions. Faced with this perception on the part of the staff, the principal tended to become even more rigid in terms of role interpretation and production emphasis. This continued the cycle that seemingly never ended.

Halpin (1966) also asserted that in a closed-climate organization people's perceptions were distorted through the selective apprehension of reality—that is, inauthentic individuals in the organization selected out or disregarded any criticism or point of view that disagreed with their own. Halpin went on to indicate that these people began to selectively distort reality and tended to group together to provide mutual support.

The description of the members of the inauthentic group closing ranks was reminiscent of Festinger, Riecken, and Schachter's (1956) description of a religious group's response to a disconfirmed prophecy. Festinger and his colleagues studied a small religious sect that predicted that the end of the world would arrive on a given date. Naturally, the disconfirmation came. The members of the religious sect were placed in a precarious situation. They could not deny the disconfirmation of the belief. They could not belittle their extensive preparation,

which included selling all their worldly goods in preparing to meet their maker. What they did, instead, was seek social support to persuade others that their central belief system was valid even though the specific date and circumstances of the prediction had not yet been validated. This was the kind of relationship Halpin (1966) described as occurring among staff members and schools characterized by inauthenticity. It is not too great an extrapolation to see how this "groupthink"— based on fabrications—could be the breeding ground for individual and collective unethical behavior.

Halpin (1966) suggested that the entire concept of authenticity could be explored in relation to three major conceptual frames of reference. The first frame of reference pertained to the *marginal person*. This conceptual framework was concerned with the person who in coming into a new milieu and desiring to be accepted in that new circumstance overconformed to the norms of his or her new peers. The fear of exposing one's difference in a new situation gave rise to embracing the group's stance on important issues and to fastidious acceptance and promulgation of the norms of the group. In doing this, the individual functioned inauthentically. The person denied something essential about himself or herself. Halpin related this concept to education in stating that education was a marginal profession characterized by modest wages and professional personnel who typically came from less-than-the-best colleges and less-than-the-best homes. Halpin asserted that teachers and administrators behaved as other marginal people did. They eagerly overconformed to what they perceived to be society's expectations for them. A specialized case of this behavior concerned the school principal. The inauthentic principal tended to overconform to what he or she viewed as the social and work stereotypes that were ascribed to the position of principal.

Halpin's (1966) second framework dealt with the difficulty of interpersonal relations in a cross-cultural exchange. In describing Perlmutter's (1959) work, Halpin suggested that teachers and administrators reacted to suggestions and criticism from the outside world in one of two ways. Perlmutter described a situation in which Americans going abroad for the first time encountered foreign cultures that were obviously different from their own. In that situation, the Americans typically employed one of two responses, especially when the foreign culture presented a dissonance-producing circumstance. For example, if a male visitor to another culture saw that men in that culture typically were refined, enjoyed the arts, and gave full vent to their emotions in public, this situation could produce a great deal of dissonance for the "All-American male." The American could reject the foreign culture as embracing men who were effeminate or allow for a subtle change in his own value system and even come to embrace some of the foreign culture he observed.

In like manner, teachers and administrators normally encounter situations in which the public criticizes their function. The reaction to this criticism can be a defensive one. On the other hand, the reaction can be an incorporation of the suggestion or criticism in an action plan for future improvement, depending, of course, on whether the suggestion or criticism is valid. Halpin (1966) suggests that the first response would be inauthentic, whereas the second response would be authentic.

The inauthentic response could likewise be viewed in terms of Festinger's (1964) *reaction formation*. In the previously described religious sect that had its end of the world prophecy disconfirmed, the members of the sect regarded outsiders (that is, anyone not belonging to their group) as profane and damned. This reaction not only served to insulate the group from the outside world, it also served to solidify the membership in its own belief system. This appeared to be the problem evident in interpersonal relations in a cross-cultural exchange.

Halpin's (1966) third framework relates Erikson's (1956) "crisis of identity." Halpin submitted that the stages a principal and his or her followers went through in moving an organization from a closed to an open organizational climate were roughly similar to the stages that a child and the child's family went through from the time of the child's infancy to the time of the child's maturity. Halpin argued that some adolescents never achieve maturity just as many school staffs never achieve a truly open organizational climate. He concluded that the conditions and behaviors mediating against the person's achieving maturity are psychologically analogous to the conditions and behaviors that maintain a closed organizational climate in its closed state.

DEFINITION OF LEADER AUTHENTICITY

Based on the classic literature from several social science disciplines and the results of the first empirical study on leader authenticity

(Henderson, 1982), I conclude that the authentic leader is distinguished by the aspects of accountability and admitting to mistakes, perceived nonmanipulation, and salience of self over role. The followers of the authentic principal see a person who is real. They see a person who accepts responsibility for his or her own actions and for the actions of those in the organization. They see someone who makes mistakes, admits them, and obviously tries not to repeat those mistakes. Their principal sometimes surprises them. The principal does not always act the way a principal is supposed to act. If a benefit would accrue to the organization through the principal's dressing differently, behaving differently, or saying things out of the ordinary, their principal is not constrained by perceived role requirements. Their principal is not viewed as a manipulator of people. Finally, there is a perceived congruence between the principal's expressions and the principal's actions. In short, this is an ethical and authentic person first and administrator second.

The followers of the inauthentic principal, on the other hand, see a person who plays everything strictly "by the book." Their principal functions in the job very much the way the job description was written but tends to maintain the effort at that routinized level. The personality of the principal is engulfed by the demands of the office. Those teachers feel that their principal not only lacks a sense of self beyond the role but also tends to deal with them on that level. Although that in and of itself is not unethical or even a breeding ground for unethical conduct, the inauthentic principal is viewed as dealing with teachers in a sterile, objectified sense. They see this principal as one who willingly would scapegoat others to "save his (or her) own neck." This leader makes no mistakes—or at least none to which the leader is willing to admit. Their principal tends to say one thing and do quite another. Subordinates view this principal as a two-dimensional being. This inauthentic principal demonstrates a clear failure of character.

Accordingly, the concept of leader authenticity is defined as the extent to which followers perceive their leader to be maximizing the acceptance of organizational and personal responsibility for actions, outcomes, and mistakes; the nonmanipulation of followers; and the salience of self over role. Leader inauthenticity is defined as the extent to which followers perceive their leader to be "passing the buck" and blaming others and circumstances for errors and outcomes, to be manipulating followers, and to be concerned primarily with operating according to the prescribed organizational role.

————————————●————————————

SUBSEQUENT AUTHENTICITY STUDIES

The concept of leader authenticity proved to be of substantial heuristic value and produced certain interesting and illuminating findings. For example, Hoy and Henderson (1983) demonstrated that leader authenticity of elementary school principals is significantly related to openness in organizational climate and to humanism in pupil-control orientation of the school. Ding (1993) examined the relationship between principal authenticity and teacher job satisfaction and found a significantly positive relationship. Given the ethical basis for the authentic principal's behavior, none of these results is particularly surprising.

Meyer (1991) examined the relationship between the concepts of perceived leader authenticity and the perceived instructional leadership behaviors of middle-level principals. Meyer identified several findings of note that once again have clear ethical overtones:

1. A good instructional manager is an accountable, highly visible supervisor of instruction who provides performance incentives to both teachers and learners without manipulation.
2. Teachers' perceptions about authenticity and instructional management differ from those of supervisors and principals.
3. Male teachers have some perceptions different from female teachers.
4. Older teachers with more years of working with the current principal perceive the principal to be more manipulative than other groups do.
5. Teachers in higher enrollment schools have higher perceptions of the frequency or quality of some principal behaviors than do teachers from smaller enrollment schools.

Lasserre (1990) examined the relationship between teachers' perceptions of the context variables of teacher interactions, principal-teacher relations, and leader authenticity and the personal variables of teacher self-efficacy and teacher self-confidence. Lasserre found a strong relationship between the context measure for school climate and the personal variable of self-efficacy. Teacher interaction is significantly related to personal teaching efficacy and principal-teacher relations are

significantly related to teaching efficacy. The perception of the teachers regarding relationships between their own personal efficacy, teaching efficacy, and total efficacy and leader authenticity were found to be statistically significant. In short, if teachers are treated in an authentic and respectful fashion they tend to treat their peers in such a manner. This enhances their sense that they can make a difference in the lives in their care. Such is the basis for ethical treatment of peers and clients.

CONCLUSION

The linkages between notions of character growth and leader's authenticity seem apparent. The school leader's selflessly working to perform in the best interest of others—internal or external organizational "clients" such as teachers, students, and parents—is a respectful act. This is directly analogous to the leader authenticity aspect of nonmanipulation. The school leader's possessing courage and a strength of character is another ethical imperative. To accept responsibility for actions and mistakes and to move to correct those difficulties is a sine qua non of effective schools. This attribute directly relates to the leader authenticity aspect of accountability. Finally, the ethical school leader exhibits the actions of servant leadership and is clearly honest—both to herself or himself and to the school's stakeholders. The ethical school leader is not a puppet but is rather a real person possessing a moral compass for the leader's expressions and actions.

The empirical evidence is clear that true authenticity of leadership in schools fosters schools in which interpersonal trust and respect, ethical behavior, and positive morale and job satisfaction predominate. Moreover—and of great importance to those who call for increased school productivity and enhanced standards—authentic behavior also results in schools in which accountability, teacher self-efficacy, effective teacher supervision, and leader effectiveness are evident. These character-based schools are places where students, teachers, and principals have a chance to model behavior that is accepting of responsibility, that exhibits a sincere concern for all members of the school community, and that demonstrates that the teachers and principals are real human beings who treat others according to their needs and not according to monolithic rules. These are schools where young people are encouraged to succeed academically and interpersonally. These are schools that build character.

REFERENCES

Bales, R. F. (1958). Task roles and social roles in problem solving groups. In E. Maccoby, T. Newcomb, & E. Hartley (Eds.), *Readings in social psychology*. New York: Holt.

Brandt, R. (Ed.). (1992). Transforming leadership [Special issue]. *Educational Leadership, 49*(5).

Burns, J. M. (1978). *Leadership*. New York: Harper & Row.

Carter, L. (1954). Recording and evaluating the performance of individuals as members of small groups. *Personnel Psychology, 7*, 477-484.

Ding, W. (1993). Relationships among principals' leadership behavior, principals' authenticity, and teacher job satisfaction in selected junior high schools (Doctoral dissertation, University of Northern Colorado, 1992). *Dissertation Abstracts International, 53*, 2617A.

Erikson, E. H. (1956). The problem of ego identity. *Journal of the American Psychoanalytic Association, 4*, 56-121.

Festinger, L. (1957). *Conflict, decision, and dissonance*. New York: Row, Peterson.

Festinger, L. (1964). *A theory of cognitive dissonance*. Stanford, CA: Stanford University Press.

Festinger, L., Riecken, H., & Schachter, S. (1956). *When prophecy fails*. Minneapolis: University of Minnesota Press.

Getzels, J. W., & Guba, E. G. (1957). Social behavior and the administrative process. *School Review, 65*, 423-441.

Halpin, A. W. (1966). *Theory and research in administration*. New York: Macmillan.

Henderson, J. (1982). Leadership authenticity: The development and validation of an operational measure (Doctoral dissertation, Rutgers University, 1981). *Dissertation Abstracts International, 43*, 993A.

Hoy, W. K., & Henderson, J. E. (1983). Pupil authenticity, school climate, and pupil-control orientation. *Alberta Journal of Educational Research, 29*, 123-130.

Lasserre, C. M. (1990). Relationships between selected school context variables and teacher self-efficacy and self-confidence (Doctoral dissertation, University of New Orleans, 1989). *Dissertation Abstracts International, 51*, 364A.

Meyer, T. M. (1991). Perceived leader authenticity as an effective indicator of perceived instructional leadership behavior in middle school principals (Doctoral dissertation, Andrews University, 1990). *Dissertation Abstracts International, 53*, 2617A.

Perlmutter, H. V. (1959). *Person to person: A psychological analysis of cross-cultural relationships*. Topeka, KS: Menninger Foundation.

8

---◆---

Making Leadership Count

ROBERT D. MYERS

Former Superintendent
Fox Chapel Area School District
Pennsylvania

"A clearly understood reality of organizational behavior is the powerful influence that a person at the top has in setting a moral tone."

—Charles E. Watson (1991, p. 132)

The Fox Chapel Area School District is located 10 miles north of Pittsburgh, Pennsylvania. The six municipalities making up the 33 square miles of the school district span a wide range of socioeconomic diversity. Although 98% white, there is evidence of a growing Asian American and African American presence in the community.

There are four elementary schools, one middle school, and one high school to serve 4,200 students. The district residents have traditionally supported and valued excellence in education, with 84% of the financial support of the school program derived from local taxes.

VISION

As the new superintendent in the Fox Chapel Area School District, I was faced with the choice of whether to maintain the status quo, as everything appeared to operate smoothly, or establish a vision involving a new direction for the district. With an average superintendent's tenure in Pennsylvania being less than 3 years, it was obvious that increased risk due to change could result in an abbreviated tenure as superintendent. I decided to take that risk, based on my years of service in the district and the knowledge that internal workings of the district needed to be revised to maximize the potential of teachers, administrators, and students.

Bolman and Deal (1994) write in *Leading With Soul,* "Heart, hope, and faith, rooted in soul and spirit, are necessary for today's managers to become tomorrow's leaders, for today's sterile bureaucracies to become tomorrow's communities of meaning, and for our society to rediscover its ethical and spiritual center" (p. 12). Leadership is necessary, whatever the degree of risk, to move an organization forward, particularly in a new direction.

One of my earliest tasks as superintendent was to convey the message that change was going to occur in all facets of the organization. An expectation was set for administrators to play a key part in moving the district forward through leadership rather than their traditional management role. To prepare staff members for their changing roles, outside consultants were engaged to focus on the process of change and to assist administrators in preparing for their new leadership roles.

I presented the new vision as "A Focus to the Future." It was a plan to prepare students for their future in the 21st century. The individual student was the intended focus in this new initiative, with students' needs to be met through a personalized approach to instruction. The new plan also placed a strong reliance on technology to assist the process of individualized instruction and, finally, the development of leadership among all administrative and teaching staff through site-based decision making and the development of a conscious awareness of ethical behavior on the part of all stakeholders involved with the school district.

This blueprint provided the framework for future consensus building and served as the foundation for the strategic planning process that followed. More important, the issue of character development and ethical thinking was elevated to a level of conscious awareness in an effort to influence all elements of our thinking in the district.

PARADIGM

I had served 14 years as the district's high school principal and 2 years as assistant superintendent before moving to the position of superintendent, a position that I held for 5 years. From my earlier administrative experience, it was increasingly apparent that the moral compass needed by many young people to guide their decisions was out of alignment.

For example, an increasing use of profanity and vulgarity was observed among both boys and girls. One particular incident prompted the suspension of a football player, although his parents saw absolutely nothing wrong with such behavior. Indeed, they expressed the belief that there was something wrong with the principal for suspending their son.

In another situation, a sophomore female student, whom I was interviewing about her suspected use of marijuana, expressed concern over the double standards of adults. She confided that her parents raised marijuana plants in the basement of their home for personal use.

Another illustration of a growing problem was observed at a movie theater. While I was waiting for the doors to open for a weekend matinee, an automobile discharged two boys about 6 and 8 years of age in front of the theater. In conversation, the children reported to me that their parents had "something to do," so the children were dropped off at the movie theater. They said that they were going to see a movie that was R-rated. When I asked how they could be permitted to enter, they said that theater personnel had not questioned them when, also unaccompanied by parents, they earlier attended an R-rated version of the same movie they planned to see that day.

One could generate a long list of anecdotes concerning children and young adults that confirm that there is something inherently wrong with our society. Charles E. Watson reported in his book *Managing With Integrity,* "The Josephson Institute of Ethics published a 1990 report on the ethics of youth with the alarming conclusion that young people in unprecedented proportions have severed themselves from the traditional moral anchors of American Society—honesty, respect for others, personal responsibility, and civic duty" (p. 10). From the corporate level to preschoolers, there is evidence that the United States is becoming morally bankrupt.

The questions one must ask are:

- Does anyone care that as a nation we are becoming morally bankrupt? Should we care?
- Do individuals in a position of leadership in an organization have a responsibility and a role to help develop ethical or value constructs for the constituent groups in the organization?
- What are the implications for school leaders in addressing these issues?

For the sake of our youth, our country, and our society, leaders must care and recognize that they do have a responsibility. The rudderless ship drifting about without the traditional moral anchors and moral compass must be retrofitted. Individuals in leadership positions can make it happen. At the very least, they can toss the first pebble in the pond to cause the ripples to occur.

CONSENSUS

Ethical behavior, character, values education, and anything with a similar title are issues rooted in controversy. I anticipated that the initiation of a program dealing with the topic of ethics in the school program could spark a major controversy in the community. There was an obvious need to develop support from the community and staff.

To accomplish this, a forum was planned and conducted by the district involving residents, parents, students, and staff who represented the cultural, racial, and religious diversity of the school district. Clergy were also invited to attend, and the meeting was held in a local church.

The agenda of the forum included the following:

1. A presentation on why a community should be concerned with ethical behavior. This discussion was intended to create a

heightened awareness of the need for a focus on ethical behavior in the schools to benefit the community.

2. A presentation by the staff of the Center for Character Education, Civic Responsibility, and Teaching from Duquesne University. This presentation was intended to share ideas on an integrated approach to character education in schools.
3. A discussion to determine how ethics might be approached in the school program, community at large, and church organizations. This discussion was intended to illustrate that ethical behavior is a community and societal concern and not just a school issue. A definition of ethics was promulgated and recommendations were offered for how the issue of ethical behavior should be addressed.

As a result of the forum, it was determined that the topic of ethical behavior needed to be addressed in the district's vision and mission statements and the district's strategic plan, which were in an early stage of preparation. Additionally, in the church organizations it was determined that the clergy needed to address the issue of ethical behavior with their respective congregations. There was general recognition that the schools could not do the job alone.

Following the forum, the school district served as a catalyst for the clergy to reactivate the local Network of Churches, which had not met for several years. Debate followed over how to define ethical behavior and what was encompassed in teaching about ethics.

A rabbi recommended the group consider the tenets of *A Lesson of Values: A Joint Statement on Moral Education in the Public Schools,* issued in May 1990 by the Synagogue Council of America and the National Conference of Catholic Bishops. The lexicon of values included justice, compassion, honesty, respect for oneself, respect for life, respect for others, freedom and responsibility, and peacemaking.

During succeeding meetings the ministerium continued to discuss one of the values at each meeting. Some clergy also addressed the issue of ethical behavior in sermons in support of the school district's effort.

As the district's strategic planning process proceeded under the guidance of the assistant superintendent, there was strong support for directly including ethical behavior in the strategic plan as recommended by the forum participants.

The strategic planning process produced a vision statement based on "A Focus to the Future." The following paragraphs were included in the vision statement, to be placed in the school entrance, dealing with ethical behavior.

> When you walked in this morning, past our mission statement at the front door of every building, you saw a lot going on. You happened to walk through a common area in our high school where teenagers gathered, chattering away. We thought about students' needs when we built our facilities. You possibly noticed the color in our elementary buildings, including the student artwork on the walls.
>
> One of the things that struck you about the comfortable chatter is that you didn't hear those "killer" statements which you've heard in other places. Respect is important here, as are all kinds of other ethical behaviors. Our community works with us to face broad ethical issues together. Our business office cares about the way we treat vendors, and students don't need to cheat anymore. They understand that they don't have to be better than someone else to be the best they can be.

The mission statement of the district also addressed ethical behavior. The mission statement is as follows:

> Our mission, supported by a commitment to excellence,
> is to educate citizens who can reach in for ethical behavior,
> reach up for quality, reach another for service, reach
> together for the good of the whole, reach each other for
> mutual respect, and reach out for lifelong learning.
> Such citizens can change a nation.

To accomplish this mission, it was determined that the district needed to focus its energy on

- Diversity/Inclusion/Gender—consistently addressed in curriculum, hiring, and self-esteem
- Ethical Behavior—pervasive in the ways we organize, model, and treat each other
- School and Community—global and local partners together
- Student Involvement—every student—sports, service, learning, leadership

- Responsibility—for learning, for behavior, for each other
- Resources—financial, human, technology—use what we have
- Learning—well taught and lifelong
- Centering—logic, planning, questioning
- Risk—dare to design a future that does not yet exist
- Communication—often and in a variety of ways

The strategic plan included eight goal areas with accompanying strategic directions. The goal statement for ethical behavior, a direct outcome of the forum, reads,

Every student will adopt and model a personal code which embodies the transmission of positive cultural principles which reflect the shared beliefs of a civilized order, ethnic traditions, and family values, including a sense of right and wrong, respect for self and others, and the rules one believes in and lives by. It requires participation which contributes to the quality of life of the individual and the entire human family.

The strategic direction stated,

We will create an environment that fosters and supports ethical behavior at all levels, including administration, instructional staff, pupil services, support staff, students, and community by:

- providing opportunities for students to develop sensitivity, respect, and concern for all people and to recognize their commonalities;
- integrating ethics education fully into all courses throughout all grade levels;
- developing school-based programs planned to promote ethical behavior, and that includes a focus on acceptance of self and others; and
- providing quality staff development and appropriate behavior through codes of ethics.

The strategic plan was adopted a year following the forum designed to develop consensus support for addressing the topic of ethics in the school environment. In retrospect, it is clear that it would not have been possible to infuse the plan with the issue of ethical behavior without the forum and the support of the forum participants, especially residents, parents, and clergy. Consensus building was a key factor in moving forward.

THE DISTRICT TODAY

Following the adoption of the strategic plan, one of the first overt manifestations of the seriousness of addressing ethical behavior was to encourage the Board of School Directors to adopt a code of ethics as a policy. After considerable discussion, the board adopted the ethics statement of the Pennsylvania School Boards Association, which was subsequently displayed in the board meeting room. Administrators adopted and displayed the ethics statement of the American Association of School Administrators on a plaque in their offices. Large posters with the vision and mission statements were signed by all staff in each building and prominently displayed at the school entrances to encourage a strong commitment to the values of the organization. Although the act of adopting and displaying statements of ethics might be questioned by some, the event was a visible and symbolic reminder to all that the district was serious about high principles of ethical behavior. The challenge for all was to live and act by the principles rather than just read the words.

Buildings were responsible for developing action plans based on the district strategic plan. Codes of behavior were promulgated in each building for students based on the district's philosophy of positive character development. One building site team researched the Heartwood Institute's (1993) character education curriculum. This literature-based program involves stories with ethical content. The stories are based on the universal attributes of courage, loyalty, justice, respect, hope, honesty, and love.

Parents and staff strongly supported the Heartwood project and it expanded to each of the elementary schools and the middle school. About a year following the adoption of the Heartwood project, there was an attack leveled at the program by a resident during a school board meeting. The response of parents in support of the Heartwood project at the next month's board meeting was overwhelming. The

Heartwood project is firmly established as part of the Fox Chapel Area School District's program on ethics education.

Each school site continues to address the issue of ethics education as it prefers under the aegis of the district's strategic plan. One school, for example, developed the Everyday Heroes Program in cooperation with the local Optimist Club, area businesses, and the local newspaper. Students are recognized in the newspaper for good deeds they perform. The program now embraces all the district's elementary schools.

Meetings have been held regularly with the various constituent groups of the six municipalities constituting the district, including the mayors; chiefs of police; clergy; and representatives of professional, service, and business organizations. A districtwide organization, All of Us Care, has emerged as a major community-based initiative to support the efforts of the school district. The organization has expanded its agenda to exert a major positive influence on the quality of life of the entire community. It will also play a role in heightening the entire community's awareness of appropriate ethical behavior.

CONCLUSION

Clearly, the leadership role of the superintendent, administrative and teaching staff, and Board of School Directors is key to the development of a high-quality school system. Five of the six buildings have been recognized as national Blue Ribbon Schools by the U.S. Department of Education during my tenure as superintendent and a host of other state and regional honors have been accorded to the district as well.

Leadership does establish the tone and policies for what happens in an organization such as a school district, whether at the district or building level. Leadership at all levels has been responsible for an abundance of meaningful change in a relatively short period of time. The person at the top, however, bears a direct responsibility for establishing the moral tone and the vision for the organization. What has occurred in the Fox Chapel Area School District has moved us closer to discovering our ethical and spiritual center. More important, however, is that we will be educating citizens, as our mission statement indicates, who can change a nation.

REFERENCES

Bolman, L. G., & Deal, T. E. (1994). *Leading with soul.* San Francisco: Jossey-Bass.

Heartwood Institute. (1993). *Heartwood: An ethics curriculum for children.* (Available from the Heartwood Institute, 465 N. Craig St., Pittsburgh, PA 15213).

Synagogue Council of America and the National Conference of Catholic Bishops. (1990, May). *A lesson of values: A joint statement on moral education in the public schools.*

Watson, C. E. (1991). *Managing with integrity.* New York: Praeger.

Principle Five

Empowered Teachers Promote
Character Development

9

Constructing Learning and Character

FRANK M. RIBICH

Professor and Chair
Department of Educational Services
Duquesne University

"If you ask what is the good of education, the answer is easy—that education makes good people and that good people act nobly."

—Plato

L ife is not value free. Behavior is not devoid of moral, ethical, or value-driven choices. Acceptance of these propositions suggests that the development of character must play a profound role in the education of our children. Teachers, by virtue of their position in the school, are empowered to provide opportunities and the necessary resources for their students to develop meaningful behaviors and attitudes so that they can use their insights and experiences to make better cognitive and affective decisions.

Teachers who see themselves as empowered are generally the most respected members of the faculty. They model positive and constructive behavior for their students and their peers. They are confident in their ability to breed success, are good at what they do, and always seek ways to improve.

The constructivist view suggests that each person has the power for personal and professional development and the capacity to empower others. In this view, the person is the natural place to focus attention because the quest for growth and development is a subjective inclination, an attitude that seeks itself.

THE ROOTS OF CONSTRUCTIVISM

Constructivism is grounded in the philosophy and psychology of phenomenology. In the broadest sense, phenomenology can be described as the lived quality of inner experience of the individual: how he or she perceives the external world and reacts to those perceptions (Giorgi, 1975). The content is in the phenomena of experience. The process suggests a personal dialogue with the perceptions of experience. The individual comes to know the world by interacting with it and uses the operative cognitive structure to reflect on and explain experience.

Yet, cognition does not exist in a void; affect is also critical in the development of meaning because of the intentionality of behavior. Learning is an active process that requires attention and will.

Phenomenology, then, considers behavior as meaningful human action that is intentional toward the world, that acts on the world, and that reveals the world. There must be a unity of the perceiving act and the perceived object. Consciousness is raised not by seeing an object but by seeing that we see that we are seeing the object (Kvale & Grenness, 1975). The self is an instrument of determination and a powerful factor in choice and will in given contexts (Mishler, 1979). Allport (1962) suggests that humans are not just "reactive" to past causes but also "proactive" in terms of using that past to create for the future. This notion suggests that for a person to truly construct meaning, that person must also be afforded the opportunity to think and reflect on his or her own actions—actions that contain knowledge (cognition) and values (Rogers, 1961).

The self is the most important part of one's phenomenal field. Perceptions are organized around it. Perceptions are influenced by needs, beliefs, and attitudes and represent an enormously rich source of data. It is reasonable to assume that our perceptions of the world are significantly influenced by the perception of self. Phenix (1977) states, "Being is a projection of self into the future. . . . A person does not absorb independent values from outside the self" (p. 65). It seems, then, that taking internal frames of reference is important to understanding the self and important to understanding the subjectivity of others.

The normal person, free from threatening conditions, can strive for unity. Learning of the power of the self increases potential and confidence to control the environment in which thinking, acting, and feeling take place. Understanding the self as an instrument of learning impacts significantly on one's perception of competence and worth.

Given the foregoing constructivist perspective, the teacher plays a profound role in the development of character of each student. The constructivist teacher opens pathways for students to be and become in their own right. Students are encouraged to seek in the life-world in their own meaningful way, exploring their own style, taking risks, hypothesizing, and identifying what they do and do not know. To promote an environment of self-renewal, to deal with complexity and change, to deal with the person, there is a need for teachers to provide for student diversity and an expression of internal processes. There is not an absolute form of helping in the process of dealing with self-discovery, but there are measures that can emphasize individual confrontation with events. If in these events students realize they are subjects and meaning given to anything is given by them, then meaning becomes a dynamic that is created and changed, and learning emerges. Students who, for example, are asked to construct projects that solve problems are apt to gain greater meaning from this learning experience than students who are told the answers or given the solution. This art form requires practice in reflectivity and the implementation of new and different patterns of behavior; it requires emphasis on presenting students with inventive and constructive experiences. There are elements of experience that need reflection and criticism.

Phenix (1977) suggests that deliberative reflection produces a "rational affect" because reason seems to be the best ally of affect. The function of reason is to consider the relationships among affects. Affect and reason are oriented essentially to the individual in his or her activity environment. If the behaviors in the activity environment are determined by the self's phenomenal field, then to understand the self with some confidence, one needs to know the phenomenal field. Understanding that the self is the instrument of learning provides for a significant impact on one's sense of competence and worth. The self-instrument can and will reconstruct experience between goals and ends, develop new meanings, and direct new experiences.

Rogers (1969) asserts that the essence of teaching is the relationship between the teacher and the student. The facilitation of learning depends on "attitudinal qualities" in the personal relationship between the facilitator and the learner. The "attitudinal quality" in the phenomenological sense refers to being. Teachers must reflect their own subjectivity and their own being to model the phenomenal agents they should be. Authenticity only develops from the authenticity of teachers who encourage students in the context of growth and who share, mediate, and dialogue with students.

Empowered teachers, in the phenomenological sense, are more participants than instructors. They help students move toward becoming reflective in their own right. They guide students to construct their own experiences—to develop awareness of what there is to learn, what they have learned, what they need to learn, and what they want to learn. Learning does not reduce itself to a specific content. The content must be understood in terms of the biography of the learner and his or her way of perceiving the task. Learners' perceptions can be expressed as knowledge, application, and attitude.

Teachers with a constructivist vision utilize the classroom context to explore student concerns and questions. In this context and its attendant processes, a semblance of order in the students' inner world is developed. This perceptual order is shareable and serves as the basis for new orders. There is a value, then, in an unending creative revision and sophistication of order through reflective activities and through projection of being into the future. When the goal of pedagogy is the construction of being, one not only comes to value the accepted being, one presumes progressive possibility.

Basic to constructivist pedagogy, therefore, is the use of the self as the technological base. The self is the owner of the experience. He or she should be able to come to share the phenomena of the experience, his or her ownership. Students must be able to speak of themselves in a precise awareness of what is owned. To be understood in their own right, they must be able to describe in a well-informed and well-grounded way their behaviors in the experience.

Education literally means "to lead out" or "to bring out latent capabilities." *Capabilities* must of necessity include the development of appropriate ethical, moral, and values-driven behavior. This simple concept underscores what teachers have always recognized intuitively—that teaching involves more than the distribution of information, and that teachers are responsible for the development of the whole child.

IMPLEMENTING A CONSTRUCTIVIST VIEW

Teachers who actualize the constructivist viewpoint empower themselves to empower their students. They become more productive and more effective when they see themselves and their work as contributing fundamentally to the growth of others. Empowered teachers promote independence, self-worth, decision making, reflectivity, and collaboration. Most of all, such teachers guide students to conceptualize all the possibilities in their development, to see means and ends, to establish relationships, and to construct the meaning of experiences.

Empowered teachers structure curriculum and pedagogy so that there is a clear relationship between ends and means. They recognize that the curriculum is more than a piece of paper. It is the product of human thought and requires integration through interaction, assuming that we come to know our world by interacting with it and use our operative cognitive structure to explain what we have experienced. From a constructivist perspective, content and process are inseparable and shareable and therefore there is active involvement in understanding subjective interaction with phenomena (McCown, Driscoll, & Roop, 1996).

Facilitating student development requires viewing students as persons and as learners through the students' reflective language as well as their products because the students are the major participants in their experience. The dialectic, or investigation of truths by systematic reasoning, between the initiation of tasks and the ultimate results belongs to the students. The meaning that is generated in the dialectic is the true matter of education because meaning expresses notions about capability, perception, value orientation, problem-solving approaches, and the like. Description provides concrete manifestation of abstract phenomena. In other words, what the empowered teachers and empowered students do is not only "get" the answer or solve a problem but also recognize the way in which they constructed meaning to get the answer or solve the problem.

Empowered teachers use opportunities for communication, action, exploration, and the construction and reconstruction of meaning. They help students to view what occurs in the classroom context from the students' unique personal history, a private construction of the world, and a personal set of beliefs and values. In so doing, teachers reflect their unique values and expectations. Teachers bring an understanding of role to the context of the classroom. If teachers are willing to reflect on their own behavior and the experiential worldview they bring to the classroom, they help students to engage in similar activity. This is, indeed, a process of being in the world and becoming, a process worthy of the time and patience that it requires.

The construction elements of growth and development are found in initiative, decision making, trial and error, risk taking, and subjective judgment. Empowered teachers encourage reflective practice, historical analysis, and the explication of the meaning of events. These are the reconstruction elements of experience that challenge students to check their behavior against their own values and to test their assumptions, where the assumptions are shared, understood, and considered to be legitimate.

The following example represents the critical difference between a constructivist position and the reductionist position that has dominated practice in education: Let us say that the end (goal, product, or competence) is to get from Point X to Point Y, wherever they may be. Decisions, judgments, and initiative are necessary to make a determination about how to get to Point Y (the means of getting there). A constructivist would engage the students in the decision-making process; a reductionist would make the decisions. Nevertheless, there may be many options available regarding the means of getting there. When the students arrive at Point Y, the goal is achieved. It is done! Reductionists tend to only see the end, and they make assessments about the end without regard for the knowledge, circumstances, events, problems, or issues that it took to get there. A void exists.

A constructivist would help the students return to the task to fill the void by encouraging them to explore the phenomenon of getting to Point y. Were there problems? Did we need help? Where did we get help from? Was the choice of getting there a good one? How do we feel about the experience? What did we learn? Did the experience contribute to the development of values, such as responsibility, respect, initiative, trust, or cooperation?

The approach to empowerment in the constructivist paradigm requires assumptions and methods that value constructive and reconstructive approaches to knowledge, reflectivity, experimentalism, and means/ends integration. Empowered teachers, role models and colleagues in the process of growth and development, are devoted not only to students' acquisition of knowledge but to what it means to be as well. A fundamental pedagogical task of empowered teachers is to strengthen students' reflectivity, self-awareness, knowledge, and understanding of experience and the rules by which they acted.

Empowered teachers posit that learners are active seekers of meaning and ultimately construct meaning in given contexts (Brown, Collins, & Duguid, 1989; Culler, 1990; Cunningham, 1992; Hlynka, 1994; Spiro, Feltovich, Jachobson, & Coulson, 1991; Wittrock, 1990). Contemporary classroom techniques, such as reciprocal teaching, teaching for understanding, and cooperative learning, are the result of the constructivist rationale (Palinscar, 1986; Sharan, 1990; Slavin, 1995; Talbert & McLaughlin, 1993).

The system of schooling as we know it is grounded in a predisposition to answers, factual regurgitation, and memorization, all of which breeds a cynicism in our students at an early age. Extant reductionist processes of schooling have intentionally fostered valuing grades, M&Ms, points, and other extrinsic motivators that have little lasting value and contribute virtually nothing to understanding the importance of self.

Empowered teachers do not control or monopolize the learning environment. They facilitate social negotiation of understandings and involve students in the assessment process. Such teachers help students learn how to ask significant questions, such as "What does it mean to learn?" "How am I participating in my learning?" and "How do I know what I have learned?"

Empowered teachers are in the best position to act as role models and colleagues in character development. Empowered teachers are able to demonstrate initiative, decision making, trial and error, risk taking, and subjective judgment. These factors represent the constructive elements of growth and development. Additionally, an empowered approach encourages reflective practice, historical analysis, and the explication of the meaning of events. These represent the reconstruction element of experience. It is possible, therefore, to construct and recon-struct the relationship between the knower, knowing, and the known. The choice is clear: behavior modification or education. We must pro-mote the latter because we owe it to ourselves as striving and thinking human beings. We should not do less.

REFERENCES

Allport, G. (1962). *Pattern and growth of personality.* New York: Holt, Rinehart & Winston.

Brown, J., Collins, A., & Duguid, P. (1989). Situated cognition and the culture of learning. *Educational Researcher, 18*(1), 32-42.

Culler, J. (1990, April). *Fostering post-structural thinking.* Paper presented at the Annual Meeting of the American Educational Research Association, Boston.

Cunningham, D. (1992). Beyond educational psychology: Steps toward an edu-cational semiotic. *Educational Psychology Review, 4,* 165-194.

Giorgi, A. (1975). An application of phenomenological method on psychology. In A. Giorgi, C. Fischer, & E. Murray (Eds.), *Duquesne studies in pheno-menological psychology* (Vol. 2, pp. 82-103). Pittsburgh, PA: Duquesne Uni-versity Press.

Hlynka, D. (1994). *Writing together: Collaborative learning in the writing classroom.* New York: HarperCollins.

Kvale, S., & Grenness, C. (1975). Skinner and Sartre: Towards a radical phe-nomenology of behavior? In A. Giorgi, C. Fischer, & E. Murray (Eds.), *Duquesne studies in phenomenological psychology* (Vol. 2, pp. 38-59). Pitts-burgh, PA: Duquesne University Press.

McCown, R., Driscoll, M., & Roop, P. (1996). *Educational psychology: A learning-centered approach to classroom practice* (2nd ed.). Boston: Allyn & Bacon.

Mishler, F. (1979). Meaning in context: Is there any other kind? *Harvard Educa-tional Review, 49*(1), 1-19.

Palinscar, A. (1986). The role of dialogue in providing scaffolded instruction. *Educational Psychologist, 21,* 73-98.

Phenix, P. (1977). Perceptions of an ethicist about the affective. In L. Berman & J. Roderick (Eds.), *Feeling valuing, and the art of growing: Insights into the affective* (pp. 59-81). Washington, DC: Association for Supervision and Cur-riculum Development.

Rogers, C. (1961). *On becoming a person.* New York: Houghton Mifflin.

Rogers, C. (1969). *Freedom to learn.* Columbus, OH: Merrill.

Sharan, S. (Ed.). (1990). *Cooperative learning: Theory and research.* New York: Praeger.

Slavin, R. (1995). *Cooperative learning* (2nd ed.). Boston: Allyn & Bacon.

Spiro, R., Feltovich, P., Jachobson, M., & Coulson, R. (1991, May). Cognitive flexibility, constructivism, and hypertext: Random-access instruction for advanced acquisition in ill-structured domains. *Educational Technology, 31,* 24-33.

Talbert, J., & McLaughlin, M. (1993). Understanding teaching in context. In D. Cohen, M. McLaughlin, & J. Talbot (Eds.), *Teaching for understanding: Challenges for policy and practice* (pp. 167-206). San Francisco: Jossey-Bass.

Wittrock, M. (1990). Generative processes of comprehension. *Educational Psychologist, 24,* 345-376.

10

Fostering Character Growth

JUDY HEASLEY

Supervisor of Special Education Programs and
Principal of the Clarence Brown Education Center
Butler, Pennsylvania

*"The primary business of school is to train children in
cooperative and mutually helpful living; to foster in them the
consciousness of mutual independence."*
—John Dewey (1899)

For teachers to be effective they must be a part of the planning process and be able to take some ownership for the direction of instruction, planning, and program implementation. Teachers are on the front
line, influencing students and colleagues in countless ways, constructing experiences and helping others to focus and reflect on their in-
volvements and to find meaning in their learning. What follows is a
description of the school in which I supervise and the education system in which I work. For me, these are special places, because I work
with students who are challenged by a range of handicaps. My school
building is a K-12 school, but in Pennsylvania support is provided to

all challenged children from birth through age 21. It is my professional passion to create a learning environment that not only is supportive of their needs but also develops in each student the qualities that can make him or her a contributing part of society. The development of character is an important component of what I do because the qualities of character are those traits that also serve a person for a lifetime.

The old adage "Nothing succeeds like success" holds true for teachers as well as students. Three very different situations follow, each related not because it can change the way educators find success but because it illustrates how learning is "a private construction" of the world and how each individual involved benefits from the process.

THE SYSTEM EMPOWERS

The Intermediate Unit System in Pennsylvania is a state-operated educational agency charged with supporting and assisting local school districts to meet the needs of member districts and their students. Twenty-eight of these specialized units are organized to work cooperatively, providing services to public and private schools throughout the state. Services ranging from providing special educational department support staff in schools and maintaining homebound services to development of programs for individuals as well as continuing education courses for in-service teachers are offered by the Intermediate Unit System.

Midwestern Intermediate Unit IV in Western Pennsylvania, where I am a supervisor and principal, provides opportunities for staff to make a difference. This difference is not simply one of administrative policy but one that empowers teachers and administrators alike. More important, through this constructivist practice, I believe we have become better teachers because we have developed a community of learners where the foundations of character growth such as trust, cooperation, respect, and responsibility are manifest in our work with each other each day and, more important yet, with the children and adults that we serve. Let me give some examples of how the constructivist environment of our school and school system has helped shape the character of the special children that we serve.

A labor-management committee was established by the executive director in our intermediate unit, in cooperation with the various labor leaders, including teachers, aides, and administrators, to provide a forum for the exchange of ideas and to increase communication and collaboration in all the schools and programs in our intermediate unit. This group meets monthly and addresses such issues as employee wellness projects and health screenings, recognition for retirees, employee recognition, employee newsletters, memorial donations, critical issues surveys, establishment of a safety committee to oversee conditions in the workplace, and cooperative in-service planning. This group provides an opportunity for teachers to participate in shared decision making as it relates to each intermediate unit program, to the recognition of teachers' talents, and to the provision of high-quality service to its school districts and students.

This same intermediate unit provides a back-to-school-week "best practices" seminar planned by a committee of teachers for staff development. This is opened to member district facilities to participate. In addition, many team-building and staff development projects are undertaken throughout the year, often through teacher initiation. One teacher a year is recognized and given an award for contributions to students outside of the classroom area. These people are nominated and selected by their peers.

By encouraging shared decision making, group participation in planning, and shared responsibility for important decisions, the administration models behaviors that foster pride in accomplishment and ownership of process. By adopting as their symbol the starfish, the staff and administration are sending a clear message that any foot can take a lead and direct the organization in significant change. A small gold starfish is worn with pride by teachers and administrators alike.

This "bottom-up" approach to the administration of our school and system has created a productive environment that addresses the most basic elements of character. Issues such as cooperation, trust, respect, and responsibility are fueled by a process, not by an autocratic individual. We are productive and sought after by schools and families because our workplace acts as a platform from which we transmit the very values that we cherish in our system. We have found that we replicate in our classrooms that type of supportive environment that we see in the administrative phases of our school system. Classrooms of students needing intensive emotional support and others with students who are multihandicapped have reaped the benefits of this philosophy.

———————————●———————————

A BUILDING IN CHANGE

One special education center in this intermediate unit has taken the first steps toward fostering a cooperative, interactive, action education. Made up of two distinct populations, multihandicapped life skills students and emotionally disturbed students, the center serves a variety of students ages 5 through 21. Staff members are certified special education teachers, but each has distinctly different experiences dealing with children and brings this expertise to the programs. Individual staff initiative is encouraged and respected.

One of the activities that have helped develop the spirit of the school has been joint planning, in which all staff members are invited to participate in designing monthly themes for instruction. Teachers then present these themes to students who elaborate on how they may contribute to the design and development of the thematic unit. Students often are involved in out-of-school activities or have family members or friends who may contribute to the lessons and theme of the instructional unit. Some students, for example, help design signs or bulletin boards; others suggest field trips or partnerships with outside organizations. This technique helps each student identify more closely with the learning that is prepared by the teacher and leads to heightened interest on the part of all the participants. This technique creates a learning environment that promotes participation and constructs meaning by getting students to invest in their own learning.

The full-time emotional support programs operated by this intermediate unit stress collaborative teaming between the unit teachers, mental health agencies, and school district staffs to provide an integrated educational and therapeutic program. The academic curriculum is consistent with local district graduation requirements, but the staff places particular emphasis on an intensive behavioral component that includes social skills training, development of decision-making processes, conflict resolution, and aggression reduction training. Teachers stress positive behavior management systems, which include parent, district, and agency cooperation and encourage students to make good decisions.

Additionally, the nature of the school environment warrants the need for teachers to cooperatively consult and work with a range of support personnel. These include professionals who are not directly in the teaching profession such as those who offer therapeutic staff support, psychiatric consultation, and mobile mental health therapy, as well as the students' individual physicians. Cooperation and communication among all these constituents are important in providing a comprehensive program for the students. In this context of shared decision making, teachers strive to encourage students to make both academic and behavioral decisions that benefit them and allow them to progress and, we hope, succeed in returning to more inclusive educational settings.

The concept of teachers helping students focus on their own progress is designed to produce cognitive shifts in the students' behaviors. This tactic is aimed at promoting positive behaviors in the students through discussion, active learning with choices, and general involvement with the learning environment. With this approach, suspensions are infrequent and used only for the most severe infractions of rules. All students are encouraged through their personal goals and behavioral expectations to develop to the best of their potential.

Working from the premise that motivation ultimately comes from within and is often determined by an individual's needs, teachers strive to promote learning situations that meet both students' and teachers' learning needs. In this approach, the teacher and student become one as they work, decide, try, err, and triumph together. Personal growth, emotional growth, problem solving, and interaction with one's environment are at once catalysts for and results of education.

In this constructive learning environment, teachers continually strive to keep current with best practices through professional organization participation and publications, attending a variety of seminars and workshops they feel pertain to their needs, maintaining university affiliations, and surfing the "net" for current research, networking, local resources, and funding sources.

Teachers are utilizing service learning throughout the programs to provide students with opportunities to plan projects, expand their learning basis, and make contributions to their community. Involvement with Clarion State University and the Keystone Smiles Americorps project has allowed teachers to develop partnerships with Habitat for Humanity, where students work on building housing; the local humane society, where they have done caretaking for animals; a local nursing home, where students helped in a bowling tournament by assisting patients in wheelchairs; a district Parent Teacher Association project in which students helped clip soup labels; a local drop-in youth center, where students participated in a local construction project; and the Meals on Wheels Program, for which our students created and donated cards and art projects for distribution to senior citizens.

Teachers helped students plan projects to improve the school facility. One classroom remodeled its bathroom, one recovered chairs, and one started a school newspaper. In addition, teachers have led a group of students to organize the school's small library.

Teachers who take the initiative to involve their students in these projects have found the projects a valuable tool to motivate and instruct and to develop problem-solving and social skills along with a real sense of accomplishment. The reflection that takes place at the completion of a task allows both teachers and students to synthesize how their learning and environments are enmeshed and how important it is to be able to trust and communicate with others. What is important is that we are living the very values that create productive individuals in society. Cooperation, trust, hope, respect, and responsibility—the elements that form character—are woven throughout these activities and projects. We see this environment as fundamental to personal growth.

AN INDIVIDUAL LOOK

Anna worked as a teacher of the visually impaired in an early intervention program in our intermediate unit. Her student, whom I will call Bobby, was a 3-year-old child who was totally blind. But there was immediate chemistry between the two—Anna saw a child with opportunities to grow, develop, and function in a sighted world, and Bobby realized something or someone was intruding in his small universe.

Knowing that nowhere are the opportunities for communication, action, exploration, and gradual awareness of meaning more natural than in the interactions between an adult and a toddler, Anna took a major role in influencing a young life. She recognized this as being especially true if the child has some sensory impairment and must rely on other modalities for information. Teaching this child became a labor of love. Anna began with planned explorations of developmental activities that other children experienced randomly. Touching, feeling, tasting, and manipulating toys and other common objects became games to Bobby, and as he grew he questioned everything. Anna was his sounding board and as he grew they began talking about the when, where, and why of everything. Once Bobby entered kindergarten, he would describe what he thought, felt, or heard and would ask many questions with a candor found only in relationships of trust. No topic was avoided, from the puzzlement of arithmetic to the mysteries of girls and how to make friends with other kids and "fit in." Many hours were spent consulting with Bobby's other teachers to plan how to use specialized techniques in his integrated setting.

Anna helped Bobby to learn at home and in his classroom, helped his teachers and classmates to understand and accept his special needs, and worked with him to make each classroom activity mean something relative to his understanding and interests.

This relationship between teacher and student lasted through Bobby's completion of the eighth grade, when he and his family moved to another state. Someone once described Anna as Bobby's lifeline, but the opposite was also true. Anna's ability to plan for Bobby, interact in many areas of his life, and relate in such a personal way allowed her to understand his academic and emotional needs and allowed her to constantly reassess and modify materials, content, and approaches to provide for the whole student. Bobby knew he could count on Anna to be honest with him, as a demanding teacher but one who allowed him to explore his options, his experiences, and his horizons.

Anna worked with many children during the time she worked with Bobby. Outside of his immediate family and our school, her work with Bobby went largely unrecognized. She extended herself and committed a large part of her professional and private life to the nurturing and development of this child, but in a very real way she had to make a difference with Bobby, because Bobby was an extension of the environment that fueled this special teacher's professional life. Our organizational structure promotes independence, cooperation, responsibility, and hope, and these positive character traits carried over into her program. This teacher, like many in our intermediate unit, sees her role in education as helping to prepare students to live responsible and productive lives. The teacher helped by constructing an environment of learning that fosters both social and academic growth. It is an environment that builds character.

———————————●———————————

SUMMARY

What makes a teacher special? What qualities do those teachers have that allow others to identify them as "wonderful," "great," "effective," "inspiring, "leaders among peers," "respected," and "good teachers"? Pick a typical faculty room in any school and listen to the dialogue. The numbers of ideas, suggestions, and reports on current projects and activities give an indication of the untapped talent and potential in any school district. Teachers need to make a difference but often lack the means to follow through on great ideas. Support, encouragement, and ownership are all critical components that determine if a project will fly.

Administrative support and school board backing are necessary for any project to succeed. For matters involving insurance and liability, it is important to consult the school's legal counsel. It is critical to do advance planning, establishing criteria for agencies participating, addressing safety issues, and establishing operating procedures at the beginning of a project. Frequent and open communication among staff, administration, and other participants is critical. Constantly reassessing goals, methods, and achievements helps to keep everyone focused and promotes success.

Most important is the individual teacher. Working in an environment where all are part of a process, where all participate in decision making, and where all are enfranchised fosters a community with the knowledge, commitment, expertise, and leadership that can change entire systems and produce remarkable results. These are the tools that build values, that can empower teachers and foster character growth in us all.

———————————●———————————

REFERENCE

Dewey, J. (1899). *The school and society.*

Principle Six

The School and Community Are Vital Partners in Developing Character

11

Community, Character, and Schooling

V. ROBERT AGOSTINO

Professor of Education
Duquesne University

"The ability to think straight, some knowledge of the past, some vision of the future, some skill to do useful service, some urge to fit that service into the well-being of the community—these are the vital things education must try to produce."

—Virginia Gildersleeve (1954, p. 34)

This chapter presents an analysis of character development in two American historical contexts. These exemplars are the Puritan community in New England, 1620-1660, and John Dewey's Chicago circa 1900. We trace with these examples the evolving relationships of school, citizenship, character, and community that have a profound effect on how we look at schools and communities today. This chapter links to the following chapter, which deals with contemporary character education in a typical suburban public school district.

--------------------------------◆--------------------------------

THE ROOTS OF CHARACTER

Character development in the New England Puritan settlements involved a three-level hierarchy. The first level was the patriarchal family structure. The Old Testament patriarch was the model for the Puritan father. He was responsible for educating and enforcing a moral code that was totally imposed by the Puritan community. The father was responsible for the salvation of his family, and his own prospects for salvation were gauged by the conduct of his family as well as his own obedience to the community.

Cotton Mather gives us a glimpse of this harsh and sometimes bewildering line of thinking that wove together the Puritan community. He wrote of a father banishing a wayward son from the dinner table, knowing that the boy would understand that being away from the father's circle was to be tilted toward destruction in the community. Edward Morgan, in *The Puritan Family* (1966), wrote of the father's responsibility to marry his daughters to men who would ensure their salvation. Morgan quoted the oddly contemporary Pilgrim saying, "Make sure of salvation and hope for riches," as advice given to marriageable maidens (p. 80).

The second level of character came from the church. Only when a family could not or would not resolve its moral problems would the minister be involved. Learning the scripture, catechism, and rules of the church justified literacy training, which in turn strengthened the character education of the home. The marathon religious services, the monitoring of each individual's behavior by others in the community, and the omnipresent minister all combined to limit the presence or practice of evil in the Puritan religious community.

The third and least important level of moral input came from the civil community. Writing in the 17th century, Thomas Hooker (quoted in Morgan, 1966, p. 1) described the civil man who obeyed all the laws, helped his neighbors, lived an admirable public life, worked hard, and prospered economically but yet was absolutely doomed to Hell! It is difficult today to understand how this paragon of civic virtue—this em-

bodiment of a civics teacher's dream—would be doomed, but to the Puritans of the 1630s he was too much of this earth and not enough of Heaven. The improper emphasis showed defective education.

These three levels came together in several ways. The choice of a marriage partner, for example, was a family, religious, and civil matter. The placement of a young girl or boy in an apprenticeship setting was a tri-level decision. The kind of work a man did in life was subject to all three levels of ratification.

This three-level system also appeared in the 1642 "Olde Deluder Satan" Act, and subsequent education statutes from the General Court of Massachusetts were enacted to ensure that the children in the town schools were being raised in the ways and tools of salvation. Religious teaching, writing, and ciphering were now carefully reviewed by a group of town selectmen. This first school board consisted of the minister and prominent men of the community. We can picture pupils of these one-room nongraded schools lined up around the town square while the town leaders quizzed them on scripture and literature and practical mathematics. Failure to do well in school was assessed by the community as a moral weakness that reflected adversely on the child's parents and home training and only secondarily as a civic or educational matter.

We find the moral residue of this thinking in U.S. society today. In his book *The Great School Legend* (1972), Colin Greer argues that many Americans continue to point to the failure of certain ethnic or racial or language groups to pull themselves up by the ladder of educational opportunity as proof somehow of defective motivation if not actual moral weakness! The Massachusetts Puritans would have understood the accusation as it applied to individuals and families. They punished nonachievers and banished nonconformists.

We continue to see this interaction today in our society and schools. Critics often link ineffective schools to the dysfunctional communities that they try to serve. Likewise, successful schools are associated with active, vibrant, moral communities that support them. The town selectmen of the Puritan communities held much the same authority that school boards have today, approving or disapproving almost everything from textbooks to teachers. The Puritans of the 17th century would recognize the matrix of values that catalyze the moral strength of one school system and the absence of which can be inferred from the failure of some other school systems. Early Puritan colonial experiences suggest several ideas that we hold about society today:

- Demographic changes alter the character of communities; larger communities inevitably differ from their antecedent groups.
- Communities sustain themselves by agreement about values and goals.
- Character is the suite of attitudes, behaviors, values, and beliefs that allow goals to be pursued and achieved.
- The geographic element binding communities has weakened and been supplanted by other linking systems, especially communication systems. For example, an ethnic or religious group need not be confined to a geographic area. Catholic or Jewish "communities" may be dispersed throughout a geographic area yet maintain viable community values through communication systems.

This early history links strongly to the principles of the integrated approach to character development. The Puritans clearly saw moral education as the pervasive matrix of all learning. Although they did not regard the civil community as an equal partner with the family or the church, they did recognize a hierarchical relation. They saw character as a dual result of abstract religious training and practical, everyday applications. This example shows us the historical continuity of approaches and ideas that the Integrated Character Development Project advocates today (Burrett & Rusnak, 1993).

These are attitudes that can be traced to our Puritan roots, when communities were determined to foster character growth through their schools.

THE NEW SCHOOL

The concepts of change, community, and education merged in the work of John Dewey in the late 19th and early 20th centuries. John Dewey was born in 1859 in rural Vermont and died in 1952. As a child, he was exposed to the pervasive influence of a residual Puritanism, Calvinism, and Congregationalism in a small-town environment.

In 1896, he established the Laboratory School, an experimental school at the University of Chicago. The span between his birth and the Laboratory School's beginning saw the end of rural, agrarian, populist values as the dominant force in U.S. community life. The span of his life after World War I saw the inexorable rise to world power of the United States. The impact on U.S. concepts and practice of "community" and "character" were equally drastic and inexorable.

Dewey experienced the reality of large demographic changes in Chicago due to southern and eastern European immigration. He anticipated what the census of 1920 showed: More than 50% of Americans in 1920 lived in urban or suburban settings. In his writings, Dewey often explored what school systems could do to replicate an adapted version of the best agricultural and small-town value systems and communities he knew from growing up in Vermont and teaching in Oil City, Pennsylvania. Along with the politician John Peter Altgeld and the social reformer Jane Addams, John Dewey in Chicago led the education arm of the Progressive reform movements.

Dewey's notion of the character of small communities assumed a town meeting type of democratic interaction in which each individual used a pragmatic/instrumentalist, problem-solving, "practical" intelligence. His critics point out that Dewey's concept of democracy had few explicit political, economic, or sociocultural connotations, although he personally held the dignity of every individual as a high value. This ethical value distinguished Progressive theory from the older Puritanical concept of the child as a small demon who needed to be civilized and socialized by the home, church, and school.

Deweyan democracy and Deweyan communities were problem-solving mechanisms through which individuals maximized their social potential. The reconstruction of one's experience in the light of others' experience plus the value of the accumulated culture gave the learner a reservoir to draw on for social self-illumination.

Dewey proposed that the school and classroom function as real communities to the point of including a working kitchen, sewing room, and carpentry shop in the lab school. He believed that classrooms could reproduce, on a smaller scale, the values and work ethic that held together rural families and villages; that strong character was forged in the agrarian United States and could be recast in urban classrooms through these character development activities.

Character education, in the Progressive sense, was developed by such things as workshops and kitchens in classrooms, student governments in schools, strong team-building physical education activities, arts and humanities in the curriculum, and inquiry and discovery approaches to social studies and science. Dewey believed that industrialization and urbanization removed children from the closeness to nature that prior generations experienced on farms and in small towns. He believed that losing contact with the farmstead, the forge, the loom, and the mill caused children to lose contact with their community values.

Dewey did, and would, support microcommunities in our schools. Examples of these might be the Girls and Boys Clubs, the scouting movement, 4-H Clubs, and any of the many school organizations that we find in our public schools today. In all these groups, respect for self and other students came from working on projects with other children and with adults. Note that the project method advocated by William H. Kilpatrick (1939) and others had the same capacity for moral and social development as does cooperative learning, in which students of different races, genders, religions, classes, neighborhoods, and abilities can appreciate their differences through cooperative efforts.

In today's jargon, we might say that Dewey proposed a paradigm reapplication. He suggested that a system of character development that worked in small towns and frontier America could be transplanted to industrialized cities filled with immigrants. The net effect of this would be the assimilation of these new "hyphenated" Americans in a urbanized, industrialized moral and ethical network recognizable by the farming and rural populations of prior generations.

John Dewey is the philosophical father of Louis Raths, Sidney Simon, and Howard Kirshenbaum's Values Clarification Theory. The 1960s and 1970s tested classroom environment theories such as "just schools" and "just communities." These are derived from Lawrence Kohlberg's post-Dewey Moral Reasoning Theory as well as work by other researchers such as Carol Gilligan. Currently, educators' interest in everything from student courts and drug courts, in which student violators are tried, judged, and sentenced by courts and juries of their peers, to community service projects can be traced to John Dewey's recognition that character and community are woven into the fabric of our schools.

COMMUNITY, NOT GEOGRAPHY

We can cite a raft of problems besetting U.S. schools today, but none is as great as the inability of our communities to share the same values, interests, and goals with our schools. We see this drama played out many times in our society. When private or parochial schools close, it is almost always because of the lack of a financial base, due to the school's inability to identify a community from which to draw students. In public schools, the complaints are often heard that communities no longer share an identity with the schools, teachers often do not live in the communities in which they serve, and schools boards are often out of touch with the needs of the community. In both private and public education, parent-teacher groups function almost autonomously as fund-raising auxiliaries. Site-based management and community governance experiments are designed to bring the authentic community back into the value structure and the operation of the private or public school.

Schools that are recognized for their academic and social success stories have managed to maintain a value system around an identifiable community. They embody some of the same basic concepts manifested in Puritan communities. For example, exemplar public schools are almost always tied to a strong community in which school activities are linked in some way to the life of the community in general. Parents can be seen in the schools contributing to a spate of activities. Community organizations are frequently called on to volunteer time, services, and money to enrich the lives of the students. The community often identifies with the progress and achievements of the school district in general and celebrates individual achievements. The same may be said for private schools in which community and not geography link parents, teachers, and students. In these schools, the community that pays for the school is also the source of the value systems those schools reach. These communities are not geographic in nature, but they share goals, values, and interests.

We can thank John Dewey and his associates of almost a century ago for helping us understand the importance of the community in the lives of our schools. But it was the Puritans who would agree with what we know today—that is, if you find a strong community, you will find a strong school that promotes character in youth.

REFERENCES

Burrett, K., & Rusnak, T. (1993). *Integrated character education.* Bloomington, IN: Phi Delta Kappan.

Dewey, John. (1966). *Democracy and education.* New York: Free Press.

Gildersleeve, V. (1954). *Many a good crusade.* New York: Macmillan.

Gilligan, C., Ward, J. V., Taylor, J. M., & Bardige, B. (1988). *Mapping the moral domain: A contribution of women's thinking to psychological theory and education.* Cambridge, MA: Harvard University Press.

Greer, C. (1972). *The great school legend.* Boston: Viking Compass.

Kilpatrick, W. H. (1939). Dewey's influence on education. In P. A. Schlipp (Ed.), *The philosophy of John Dewey.* Evanston, IL: Northwestern University Press.

Kohlberg, L. (1976). Moral stages and moralization: The cognitive-developmental approach. In T. Lickona (Ed.), *Social issues.* New York: Holt, Rinehart & Winston.

Morgan, E. S. (1966). *The Puritan family.* New York: Harper Torchbooks.

Perkinson, H. G. (1991). *The imperfect panacea: American faith in education 1865-1990.* New York: McGraw-Hill.

Raths, L. E., Harmin, H., & Simon, S. B. (1978). *Values in teaching* (2nd ed.). Columbus, OH: Merrill.

Spring, J. (1994). *The American school 1642-1993.* New York: McGraw-Hill.

12

———————————●———————————

Partnering With the Community

DONNA K. MILANOVICH

Principal, J. E. Harrison Middle School
Baldwin-Whitehall School District
Pittsburgh, Pennsylvania

> *"Families and community members are important stake-*
> *holders in developmentally responsive middle level schools.*
> *Schools recognize and support families and community*
> *members as participants in school programs by encour-*
> *aging their roles supporting learning and honoring them as*
> *essential volunteers."*
> —National Middle School Association (1995, p. 17)

A profound trend is sweeping our nation. Parents, balancing careers and family responsibilities, have come to depend on the school to provide structure and a sound education and to instill values in their children. Middle school children, seeking to belong, come to school

AUTHOR'S NOTE: The author wishes to acknowledge all the outstanding educators who have contributed to the writing of this chapter. A special thanks to Mary Monsour, whose valued input was greatly appreciated.

needing nurturance, guidance, and socialization. To incorporate an in-trinsic value system in the educational system, community involve-ment must be included as a part of the instructional program. What qualities do we foresee in this new paradigm shift? How can we offer a full-service school for middle-level learners that incorporates respect, citizenship, and moral responsibility and builds on community-school partnerships? This is a central issue in the integrated approach to char-acter education, one that crystallizes our thinking about reviving our communities through the energy of our schools.

WORKING TOGETHER

In *Turning Points: Preparing American Youth for the 21st Century* (1989), the seminal report of the Carnegie Corporation, the Task Force on Edu-cation of Young Adolescents makes two recommendations for trans-forming middle-level education to meet today's societal challenges. The task force recommends that schools

- *Reengage families in the education of young adolescents* by giving families meaningful roles in school governance, communicating with families about the school program and student's progress, and offering families opportunities to support the learning pro-cess at home and at the school.
- *Connect schools with communities,* which together share responsi-bility for each middle grade student's success, through identify-ing service opportunities in the community, establishing part-nerships and collaborations to ensure students' access to health and social services, and using community resources to enrich the instructional program and opportunities for constructive after-school activities. (pp. 9-10)

Located in the South Hills area of Pittsburgh, the Baldwin-White-hall School District, with a student population of 4,841, is a sta-ble, middle-class, suburban community. The district covers 10 square miles and includes the communities of Baldwin Borough, Baldwin Township, and Whitehall Borough. The district has three elementary schools, one middle school, and one high school to serve the commu-nity.

In its third year as a middle school, J. E. Harrison Middle School has a population of 1,161 students in Grades 6, 7, and 8. The student ethnic background at the school is predominantly Caucasian (95%), with a small percentage of students of African American, Asian, and Hispanic descent. The percentage of the student population from low-income families is 14.09%, considerably below the state average. Through its comprehensive middle-level program, J. E. Harrison Middle School strives to meet the new challenges presented by society.

Joining the staff 4 years ago as a principal charged with creating a developmentally appropriate and responsive middle school to meet the growing needs of the school population, I realized that significant changes needed to be made to meet these goals. Since these changes would require parent and community support to be successful, it was imperative that a partnership in which school and community shared a common vision and values be forged.

Working together as a collaborative team, all constituents agreed on a mission statement that recognized the importance of students becoming contributing members of school, family, and community. As a school, we set out to incorporate the Carnegie Task Force's five essential characteristics of an effective human being. We wanted each of our students to be

- An intellectually reflective person
- A person en route to a lifetime of meaningful work
- A good citizen
- A caring and ethical individual
- A healthy person (p. 15)

These characteristics indicate strong character development. Throughout school and community programs, Harrison Middle School has embraced these ideals.

LEADERSHIP

Community membership is strengthened by the ability of its members to assume leadership roles. A leadership program was developed at our school empowering the students with leadership skills to promote an understanding of the various social roles that individuals assume in the community. This workshop, training over 200 students yearly, allows students to identify problems that exist in their school community, to choose one of these problems to be addressed by their individual team, and to prepare an activity or program in which they guide their team to resolution of the problems. The Harrison Leadership Program focuses on both the role and the responsibility of the leader.

Beyond the structured leadership program, students develop leadership skills in their school community through informal activities. Examples of these activities include peer tutoring, helper positions in the library and office, and positions as student aides for students with disabilities. One project found students collecting books to build a classroom library. They expanded that project by creating the "Acts of Disrespect" fund to which students who were disrespectful were required to donate a nickel. The money collected was donated to the library to purchase books.

Students also practice leadership skills by serving the community outside of the school. For example, one team of students organized a recycling project. Students collected paper products over a 4-week period and took responsibility for getting the products to the recycling pickup truck. The project culminated with a tour of a local recycling plant. Another group of students organized a food drive. Their goal was to collect food products to benefit needy families. The food drive raised 3,000 cans of food. Seventh-grade students participated in the Race for the Cure, a program to raise money to help fight breast cancer, and eighth-grade students volunteered to help with the Special Olympics. Finally, students at Harrison Middle School demonstrate leadership skills outside of the school as they develop ongoing relationships with personal care homes and assist a local women's shelter through a yearlong clothing drive. With the guidance of their teachers, students learn to recognize their responsibility to the larger community and assume leadership roles as they respond to this responsibility.

CHARACTER IN CLASSROOMS

Building character and responsibility in students requires an integrated curriculum that is rich in discussion as well as real-life situa-

tions. Bonnie Harshbarger, a language arts instructor, began an examination of the curriculum attached to the teaching of the play *The Diary of Anne Frank* by Frances Goodrich and Albert Hackett. Questions were raised about the ethical and moral issues in the play and the strategies required to bring these dilemmas to the students.

In preparation for the unit, Ms. Harshbarger attended a course at the Holocaust Center (United Jewish Federation) taught by Linda Hurwitz. The course covered the factual information attached to the period from 1933 to 1945 and the historical origins of anti-Semitism. Social, cultural, and personal themes emerged that were embedded in the curriculum content—the thematic issues of human and civil rights, personal responsibility, respect for others, prejudice, conscience, freedom, religious beliefs, and moral courage. Mrs. Hurwitz engaged the teachers in learning activities that confronted the moral issues of the Holocaust and involved them in ethical decision-making scenarios. She challenged the teachers to involve themselves and their students in the annual Holocaust Arts and Writing Competition and Seminar. The effect on Harrison Middle School was noticeable: Students began emulating positive characteristics.

Students of Harrison Middle School bear witness to the lessons of the Holocaust, examining its moral and ethical issues. One student's profound words at the conclusion of her research paper echo many of the students' sentiments about the Nuremberg Trials:

> Hopefully, many people have learned a valuable lesson from the Nuremberg Trials. Civilization will not tolerate such a slaughter of humanity again. As individuals, we are responsible for our behavior and actions. The indifference that was evident during the Holocaust needs to be abolished. We cannot bring back the lives that were taken by Hitler and his henchmen, but as citizens we can see that this never happens again.

Through the teaching of the Holocaust, we are attempting to plant the seeds of a moral conscience and create responsibly thinking citizens for the 21st century.

Daniel Gaser, a teacher in our school, developed a living history unit with activities that enable a personal care facility to become an extension of the regular classroom. Students visit the local facility and interview the senior citizens. The residents become the students' primary academic resource. Instead of visiting the library and collecting data, students reach out in the community to a precious, human resource, one that is not renewable. Students experience the Depression, two world wars, disease, health hazards, and medical ignorance that these people experienced. What was once a textbook history lesson transfers to a reenactment of real life as the courage and endurance of these hardships are told through the senior citizens' lives.

The development of leadership programs, community service projects, and integrated curricula offer the middle level learner opportunities to connect with the community. One way to reengage families with the school is through a strong parent organization. At Harrison Middle School, the Parent, Teacher, Student Association (PTSA) has brought parents to the school by encouraging communication. Parents are invited to become active members of the school community. This partnership does not involve financial support alone. Parents are encouraged to take part in all facets of the student learning process. As part of the membership, parents assume a leadership role in schoolwide programs such as the Drug/Alcohol Awareness Week and the Student Supplies Store. They chaperon dances, field trips, and other school-related programs. Dottie Coll, PTSA president, states, "As parents, we find that our working partnership with teachers leads to a new level of comfort and many new friendships. We are connecting names with faces and problems with solutions. We have opportunities to share our concerns and to influence issues that affect our children."

COMMUNITY ENERGY

Beyond the school, Harrison Middle School parents play an active role at the district and state PTAs. At these levels, parents serve on committees that address topics ranging from health and safety issues to legislation that directly affects the students, families, and community. Mrs. Coll feels, "It is an honor for me to participate on a state level in discussions which identify issues that affect our community; develop positions regarding standards, assessments, and accountability; and promote public dialogue of these issues."

To further engage parents, an innovative student-led parent conference program was implemented in the school. This new model was a

departure from the traditional parent-teacher conference that failed to directly involve the most important person—the student. The student-led parent conference promotes student responsibility, accountability, and ownership in the educational process.

In the student-led parent conference, the student presents to a parent or other significant adult a specially prepared portfolio containing selected work samples and student, teacher, and peer evaluations that address the academic areas as well as the student's overall citizenship and behavior. During presentations, the teacher serves as a facilitator, helping the students with their presentations and clarifying information for parents. Opportunities exist in the student-led parent conference for the student, parent, and teacher to work together to help the student set attainable goals for improvement.

Students, parents, and teachers have enthusiastically embraced the program because of the positive power and energy it generates. A wheelchair-bound grandmother of one seventh grade student was extremely impressed with the student-led parent conference that she had attended. She remarked to the teacher that even though it took considerable effort for her to come to the school, in the future she would rely less on telephone conferences and more on direct involvement at the school. The effort it took for her to attend the conference in person had made a positive impact.

Helping parents deal with adolescent issues is an essential component of the middle school program. The South Hills Area School Districts Association (SHASDA) middle school principals, along with their parent organizations, planned and organized a unique Saturday morning parenting program titled PS: Communities Linked Together. Working together, Baldwin-Whitehall, Bethel Park, Mt. Lebanon, and Peters Township School Districts combined community resources donated by local area businesses and individuals. The program included a nationally-recognized keynote speaker and a number of community leaders who shared their knowledge and expertise during workshop sessions. Focusing on the many facets of parenting, the 300 participants learned about sibling rivalry, substance abuse, and time management. They explored conflict mediation and the juvenile judicial system. Feedback from the conference was very supportive. As one parent indicated, "Parents need more help in coping . . . please plan more!" Another parent stated, "I wish there would have been this type of seminar when my child was starting middle school. . . . This is positive for the communities."

Providing a safe, drug-free atmosphere where students can socially develop is an integral part of character development. The teen center model addresses these issues as it provides an alternative to loitering in area shopping centers and emphasizes the development of friendships, respect for others, and community involvement while de-emphasizing violence and vandalism in the community. On any given Friday night at the Independence Middle School in Bethel Park, Pennsylvania, over 500 middle school students join together to play basketball, Ping-Pong, and card games; dance; watch movies; and eat. The teen center provides a place where students can discover self, learn compassion for others, and care for the physical health of the body.

One key element of the teen center is the community involvement and the role of civic pride that it develops in students. Teen centers cannot operate without cooperation and support from a variety of community groups. School districts can provide the site for the center. Local drug and alcohol task forces or recreation departments can provide funding, sponsorship, and liability insurance for the center's operation. The local police department can provide free protection with attendance of a police officer. In-kind donations are often needed as much as cash in the successful operation of a teen center. Area merchants and local vendors are more than receptive to the idea of donating food, equipment, prizes, or services to teenage consumers. It is not uncommon to see hairdressers, sports companies, and local toy stores demonstrating their products at the teen center. These types of activities open the door to potential customers, help establish the community itself as a nice place to live, reduce the risk of vandalism in the community, and enhance public support and recognition for area businesses.

Chaperons are another element of the teen center that work hand in hand with building character. This group of individuals helps develop civic responsibility in students and the adults that volunteer. At one local teen center, over 50 different chaperons have volunteered each month since the center's opening 5 years ago. These volunteers included parents, local businesspeople, former students, and senior citizens. In a 5-year span, over 30,000 volunteers have been part of the program. As Mary Monsour, former director of the Bethel Park Teen Center, stated, "Each component of the community plays an important role in the successful running of the center . . . without the entire community's involvement, the center would not prosper."

Another important link in the community-school partnership is the involvement of the health community. BodyWorks was conceived from a perception that if middle school students had a better understanding of their bodies and an opportunity to talk with health care professionals, they would make better choices. The program, sponsored by the local community hospital, is a partnership of the community, school, and parents working together to complement the curriculum as it promotes good choices for healthy habits and lifestyles.

This program models many components of character development. The medical community is a wonderful example of people helping others and putting others above self. It is a profession that models cooperation as well as caring and compassion. Examples are made real for students as the emergency room doctor explains the need for teamwork when a critically injured patient arrives at the hospital or is met at an accident site by the paramedics or helicopter medical crew. The cardiovascular surgeon explains the variety of personnel, each with special training and a different task to perform, necessary for successful open heart surgery. A radiologist explains how medical imaging equipment is used to make diagnostic assessments so that a team of physicians can make the right decision about patient care. These specialists come to the school as volunteers, sharing their dedication and commitment. Their presentations are followed by question-and-answer opportunities.

The BodyWorks theme of self-reliance challenges the students to think for themselves, rely on themselves, and ask for help when necessary. The program founder, Linda Serene, feels that the unique activities of this program and the exposure to the more than 50 dedicated health care professionals encourages students to show tolerance, compassion, and respect for others with health problems.

Partnerships can bridge the gap between corporations, school, and the community. Joy Kretzler initiated a corporation-school partnership by inviting representatives from U.S. Steel to her third-grade classroom at Paynter Elementary School in the Baldwin-Whitehall School District to discuss recycling and the uses for steel in the world today. The visitors were met with a classroom of inquisitive learners, primed with questions about environmental issues.

From the discussions, U.S. Steel invited Ms. Kretzler and the Baldwin-Whitehall School District to "adopt" a 4-acre wetland. Described as the South Taylor Project, this area was long used by local steel-making facilities as a reservoir for by-products generated from the making of steel. The care and maintenance of this area, located only 10 minutes from the school district, has primarily been left to the students of the school district and formal lessons on the care and use of the land have been incorporated throughout the K-12 curriculum.

There were many components to this unique partnership that had to be addressed before children could be allowed on this property. Liability and safety issues were discussed. Lawyers from U.S. Steel, representatives of the Baldwin-Whitehall School District, and members of the Baldwin community, at large, met to address and resolve these issues.

One significant use of this corporate-community-school partnership has been the design and construction of an outdoor classroom shelter. Services were garnered from corporate employees, educational leaders, teachers, and parents. Corporations donated the design, the scaffolding, a crane, a generator, tools, materials, and expertise to aid in building. Food was donated by local grocery chains to feed the volunteers. The local PTA donated monies to buy equipment such as hoes, shovels, microscopes, and hand lenses for the children to use while on the site.

As Ms. Kretzler has learned, if there is a need, there is a way. Partnerships bridge the gap between idea and reality. The South Taylor Project brought environmental consciousness to the children of the Baldwin-Whitehall School District by emphasizing values in a science curriculum. Students took part in the project from its inception and learned the value of cooperation, trust, and responsibility.

Another character-developing outdoor activity was organized as an environmental outing for eighth-grade students. Starting with a weekend excursion, our camping experience has grown over the past 18 years. This outdoor experience takes eighth-grade students away from the confinement of the classroom and into the woods for 3 days of environmental education. It has become so popular with the community that chaperone positions are filled 8 months before the trip begins.

The support of the community is essential in providing proper nutrition and supervision during the 3-day excursion. The teachers, 15 parents, 3 nurses, and 14 high school counselors provide 24-hour supervision and care. Police officers from the community meet with the students and answer questions. Local businesses provide incentives for the students.

Harrison Middle School students receive many benefits as the result of this program. The confidence course builds decision-making skills, courage, self-respect, and respect for others. The experienced fishing students eagerly show novices the correct way to bait a hook or cast a fly line, allowing students to interact in a caring manner. Every student carries home a special memory of camp, what teacher coordinator Steve Rowland refers to as "memories for a lifetime."

A multifaceted community program that enjoys a partnership with several community service organizations is the Drug Abuse Resistance Education (D.A.R.E.) Program. Begun 3 years ago in Baldwin-Whitehall, D.A.R.E. is supported by the Whitehall Borough Council, Whitehall Borough Police Department, Baldwin-Whitehall School District, and Whitehall business community. The uniformed police officers Bruce Marchetti and John Vitullo visit the middle school during the school day to discuss pertinent law enforcement issues. Self-respect, respect for others, and peer pressure are topics covered, with clear guidelines given to students on how to handle difficult situations. During these sessions, the officers also dispel myths about police officers and form a relationship of trust with students. The open communication has secondary effects. Students who find themselves in difficult situations often turn to one of these officers for guidance. It is not uncommon for the officers to be told, "You don't know me, but you had my younger brother in class. He told me you would tell the truth."

Public education is making great strides in building partnerships with community members. Strategic plans are being developed that identify parents and community members as essential partners in educating youth. Schools are pulling together community resources to develop a full-service program that meets the needs of all students at all levels. The total health of the student is included in curriculum materials that instill self-esteem and build self-confidence.

SHAPING THE FUTURE

Students do not learn in a vacuum; similarly, teaching does not happen in a solitary classroom. Life translates into living; real-life situations bring meaning and motivation to students. Parental input is a major component of this learning. As mentors, volunteers, and community leaders, parents hold the key to transforming the total child into a productive member of society. We, as educators, can instruct, role-model, and provide various learning activities that are developmentally appropriate. We can supply the resources for learning and evaluate the process. However, without parental support and community involvement, we fall short of our goal of educating the entire child.

As we move into the 21st century, we will see the metamorphosis of the family unit. More and more schools will be called into action as society depends on the educational system to effect an intellectually reflective human being. The school system needs to recognize this change and reengage its own attempts at holistic education. This is just the point of the integrated approach to character education—to foster learning both inside the classroom and through the community.

The future of our children rests in our hands. Although community partnerships may be costly, we must ask ourselves, "What will the cost be if we do not make these changes?" If the paradigm does not shift and the full-service school fails to become a reality, how will our youth meet the challenges of the 21st century? One powerful way to respond to this critical issue is to build the character of our children by uniting the work of our schools with the resources of our communities.

REFERENCES

Carnegie Council on Adolescent Development's Task Force on Education of Young Adolescents. (1989). *Turning points: Preparing American youth for the 21st century.* Washington, DC: Carnegie Council on Adolescent Development.

National Middle School Association. (1995). *This we believe: Developmentally responsive middle level schools.* Columbus, OH: Author.

Epilogue: Getting Started

———————●———————

PAUL F. BLACK

Professor and Chair of Secondary Education/
Foundation of Education Department
University of Pennsylvania at Slippery Rock

"During my 87 years I have witnessed a whole succession of technological revolutions. But none of them has done away with the need for character in the individual."
—Bernard M. Baruch (1957)

As you have seen in the previous chapters, the gap between theory and practice in character education is being compressed. And that is as it should be. When our forefathers and founders spoke of values, morals, civic responsibility, or character, they envisioned the manifestation of such action: "A man's character is manifest in his deeds. A woman's moral virtue is manifest in her actions." Civic responsibility meant involvement based on beliefs and corresponding action, whether those actions meant opposing increased taxation as witnessed in acts such as Shays's, Bacon's, or the Whiskey Rebellions; a belief in revolutionary ideas that was manifest in groups such as the Sons of Liberty and acts such as the Boston Tea Party; or a keener sense of participation in the democratic process such as the First or Second Continental Congress.

> Thus, the antecedents of character education began with those who knew that our nation rested on a profoundly moral idea. They were well aware that our democracy would rise or fall as a result of the citizenry's ability to respond to the moral challenge presented by this new form of government—challenges such as sitting in judgment of others in court rooms, electing just judges and representatives, and enacting ethical laws. (Ryan, 1996)

Basic to individuals meeting these moral challenges presented by society were what Ben Franklin termed virtues in his *Autobiography:*

1. Temperance
2. Silence
3. Order
4. Resolution
5. Frugality
6. Industry
7. Sincerity
8. Justice
9. Moderation
10. Cleanliness
11. Tranquillity
12. Chastity
13. Humility

Thus began the never-ending quest to identify individual and societal characteristics needed to provide a path to personal and civic responsibility. As President Clinton expressed it in his 1997 state of the union address, "Today the enduring worth of our nation lies in our values and our soaring spirit."

The instilling of values, creating a moral climate and perpetuating societal values, is a responsibility of the schools and other educational organizations. As the agents of implementation, educators share the perspective "of the great philosophers from Socrates, Plato, and Aristotle down through Kant and Dewey who stressed the importance of the moral domain in education" (Ryan, 1996). Today's character education is based on the premise that each student's moral development is as essential to the school mission as academic learning. Indeed, many leading educators see moral development as foundational to the learning process and as a key—but often neglected—element of school reform. Strong moral character is required if democratic society is to survive. The purpose of public education is to prepare its students to be good people, citizens, and workers (McKay et al., 1996).

In the last three decades of the 20th century, with the knowledge base developed by Kohlberg through his cognitive moral development process, character education has emerged. Three elements of character education are

1. It focuses on a common core of shared or universal values.
2. It is based on the belief that there are rational, objectively valid, universally accepted qualities to which people of all civilized nations, creeds, races, socioeconomic statuses, and ethnicity subscribe.
3. Its traits (qualities) transcend political persuasions as well as religious and ethnic differences.

Thus, the first obligation of a school district when it addresses character education (establishes a program or makes a commitment) is to identify the universal values that will be the focus of the program and then make a commitment to teach these core values (Wiley, 1996).

To assist school districts in identifying the core of universal values, various organizations have developed, published, and disseminated curricular materials that delineate these values. For instance, the Heartwood Curriculum offers "seven character traits":

1. Courage
2. Loyalty
3. Justice
4. Respect
5. Hope
6. Honesty
7. Love

The Character Counts Coalition identifies six pillars:

1. Trustworthiness
2. Respect
3. Responsibility
4. Fairness
5. Caring
6. Citizenship

Some school districts also stipulate their own. For example, Baltimore identifies 24 core values. St. Louis lists 50 characteristics. Dayton has a "word for the week" (Wiley, 1996). Still others present concepts that define or characterize character education, such as

1. Honesty
2. Respect
3. Responsibility
4. Concern for the underdog
5. Friendship
6. Diligence
7. Prudence
8. Caring about
9. Self-esteem
10. Trust
11. Loyalty
12. Justice
13. Commitment
14. Self-discipline
15. Self-reliance (Woodfin, Sanchez, & Scalfini, 1996)

The number of characteristics identified in these curricular models is not important, but the conceptual framework is. Furthermore, the above characteristics appear to be an extension of and in some cases similar to those outlined by Franklin in his autobiography and the wisdom offered in *Poor Richard's Almanac*.

With characteristics and concepts defined, curricular implementation is the next step. Viewpoints are divided on how this should be done. Some educational researchers have suggested that values curricula be taught directly to students in a manner similar to academic subjects like math and English; these researchers hypothesize that the constructs in the character education program must be fully understood through experience and practice before they can be completely utilized (Brooks & Kann, 1993). Other researchers argue that character education is best accomplished by weaving values into the daily curriculum. Thus, character education is not separate and apart from curriculum but an integral part of it. The editor of this book has written about this in his Phi Delta Kappa fastback. For him, character education connects intellectual and social development to purposeful learning and living. It translates ethical principles and reasoning into thoughtful decision making and responsible action (Burrett & Rusnak, 1993).

In the context of the integrated character education curriculum, the role of the teacher is to be a moral coach who cares about, reinforces, motivates, and enforces appropriate behavior and good character. In many ways, character is formed through habits of everyday living (Wiley, 1996).

Ultimately, the role of the classroom teacher and that of the school are defined or limited by the state commitment to implementing character education. The following is a summary of *state-level* activity regarding character education (this list is not intended to be comprehensive):

1. California requires it.
2. Maine, North Carolina, Oregon, and Washington have laws requiring schools to teach moral or ethics education.
3. Virginia and Louisiana have social studies standards in character and citizenship.
4. West Virginia integrates it in the content curriculum.
5. Vermont includes it in the Common Core of Learning.
6. New Hampshire does not require it in curriculum but requires each school board to develop a policy stating how character education is being taught.
7. Iowa passed a law encouraging but not mandating it.
8. Ohio provides a research guide (South Carolina is writing one).
9. Kentucky wrote a nonmandated curriculum.
10. Alaska, Kansas, Minnesota, Pennsylvania, and Texas have *no* state-level activity. (Wiley, 1996)

As states recognize the importance of character education as a discipline and incorporate it in their curricular standards, it follows that the teacher preparatory process at both the pre- and inservice levels should include character education. But this is not the case. One of the purposes of this book is to raise the consciousness of educators and the public about the need for character education to be a part of the state standards for the preparation of teachers. Let us examine the current status. Since requirements in teacher preparation programs are almost nonexistent, most teacher preparation programs in the United States do not include character education. Exceptions are New Hampshire and Washington, which incorporate character education in their standards for teacher certification requirements. Washington requires a "study of values in public schools." New Hampshire requires "character and citizenship" at both pre- and in-service levels. (In its requirements for certificate renewal, New Hampshire mandates 60 clock hours of staff development every 3 years—5 hours of which must address character and citizenship.)

Once teachers are in classrooms, a vigorous comprehensive staff development process is needed. Simply providing resource guides or curricula without staff development is the kiss of death for a new program such as character education. Without staff development, experience shows that manuals and prepackaged curricula are not used by classroom teachers (Wiley, 1996).

In summation, incorporating character education in our classrooms, teacher preparatory process, and state certification and curricular standards is going to be a long-term process that requires an ongoing dialogue about the qualities of mind and character of today's students and teachers. Together, they need to successfully navigate the complex world they will face in the 21st century. In the words of President Clinton (1997) as he outlined 10 principles in his call for action to reform U.S. education, "Principle #6: Character Education must be taught in our schools. We must teach our children to be good citizens."

To assist in the needed dialogue and to raise the level of consciousness, the Resource section provides a list of organizations that carry the torch for character education. In addition, a matrix has been developed as a ready reference for contacting organizations that publish or disseminate curricular materials (Table E.1).

Table E.1 Programs and Services

Name	Types of Materials and Curricular Topics	Availability of Materials and Cost	Prime Focus in Rank Order
Center for the Advancement of Ethics and Character	Curricular and other guidelines and recommendations; reading-literature, historical, and philosophical	Materials not for purchase but available at cost	Consulting, including conducting workshops/conferences and serving as a resource center
Center for Character Education, Civic Responsibility, and Teaching	Curricular materials K-postsecondary; philosophical, historical, and sociological	Single copies available at cost	Resource center, consulting, conducting workshops/conferences
Character Education Institute (Texas)	Curricular K-12; historical and governmental/political	In kit form ($115-$140); selected materials free of charge	Creating and publishing materials, conducting workshops/conferences, consulting
Character Education Institute (Pennsylvania)	Curricular materials K-postsecondary; reading-literature, philosophical, socio-logical, historical, governmental/political, and religious	Materials not for purchase	Consulting, conducting workshops/conferences, serving as a resource center

(continued)

Table E.1 Continued

Character Education Partnership	Curricular materials K-12	Single copy publications available free of charge and at cost	Resource center, consulting, conducting workshops/conferences, consulting
Communitarian Network	Does not publish or disseminate curricular materials		Research, workshops, organizing conferences, writing
Community of Caring (Kennedy Foundation)	Curricular K-12 in conjunction with National Association of Secondary School Principals; textbook *Growing Up Caring* distributed through Glencoe, a division of Macmillan/McGraw-Hill	Single copies of materials available at cost	Publishing materials, consulting, conducting workshops on its program
Cooperating School Districts (PREP)	Curricular K-12; wide variety	Single copy publications available at cost	Consulting, conducting workshops/conferences
Critical Thinking Books and Software	Curricular K-12 program entitled Exploring Ethics Through Children's Literature; math, history, reading, and science	Single copies of materials and publications available	Research, workshops, organizing conferences, writing
Developmental Studies Center	Curricular K-middle school; philosophical and reading-literature	Single copy publications available	Consulting, creating and publishing materials, conducting workshops/conferences

Organization	Curricular Focus	Availability	Services
Educators for Social Responsibility	Curricular K-postsecondary; math, science, and social studies	Single copies of materials available	Creating, presenting, and publishing materials; conducting workshops/conferences; consulting
Ethics Resource Center	Curricular K-postsecondary; drama and documentary videos	Single copy publications and kits available at cost	Creating and publishing materials, conducting workshops/conferences, consulting, resource center
Giraffe Project	Curricular K-12; reading-literature, sociological, governmental, philosophical, and integrated historical and scientific	Single copy publications for a fee	Creating and publishing materials, consulting, conducting workshops
Heartwood Institute	Curricular K-middle school; reading-literature	In kit form ($400-$1,000)	Creating and publishing materials, conducting workshops/conferences, consulting
Jefferson Center for Character Education	Curricular K-postsecondary via Young People's Press; reading-literature, historical, and governmental	Single copy publications and kits available at cost	Creating and publishing materials, consulting, conducting workshops/conferences

REFERENCES

Brooks, B. D., & Kann, M. E. (1993). What makes character education programs work? *Educational Leadership, 51*(3), 19-21.

Burrett, K., & Rusnak, T. (1993). *Integrated character education.* Bloomington, IN: Phi Delta Kappa.

McKay, L., Archibald G., Carr, N., & Stirling, D. (1996, Spring). Character education with personal responsibility. *Journal of Staff Development, 17*(2), 12-16.

Ryan, K. (1996, Spring). Staff development's golden opportunity in character education. *Journal of Staff Development, 17*(2), 6-9.

Wiley, L. (1996, Spring). The role of staff development in implementing character development. *Journal of Staff Development, 17*(2), 50-52.

Woodfin, D., Sanchez, K., & Scalfini, S. (1996, Spring). Community involvement jump-starts a districtwide character education program. *Journal of Staff Development, 17*(2), 24-28.

Resource:
Organizations and Programs

———————●———————

Center for the Advancement of Ethics and Character
Boston University
School of Education
605 Commonwealth Avenue
Boston, MA 02215
617-353-3262
FAX: 617-353-3924

Center for Character Education, Civic Responsibility, and Teaching
Duquesne University
School of Education
Canevin Hall
Pittsburgh, PA 15282
412-396-5193
FAX: 412-396-5585

Character Education Institute
8918 Tesoro, Suite 575
San Antonio, TX 78217-6253
1-800-284-0499
210-829-1727
FAX: 210-829-1729

Character Education Institute
California University of Pennsylvania
250 University Avenue
Box 75
California, PA 15419-1394
412-938-4500
FAX: 412-938-4156

Character Education Partnership
809 Franklin Street
Alexandria, VA 22314-4105
1-800-988-8081
703-739-9515
FAX: 703-739-4967

Communitarian Network
2130 H. Street, NW
Suite 714J
Washington, DC 20052
1-800-245-7460
FAX: 202-994-1606

Community of Caring
(Project of Joseph P. Kennedy, Jr. Foundation)
1325 G Street N.W.
Suite 500
Washington, DC 20005-3104
202-393-1251
FAX: 202-824-0200

Cooperating School Districts (PREP)
13157 Olive Spur Road
St. Louis, MO 63141
1-800-478-5684
314-576-3535 x 130
FAX: 314-576-4996

Critical Thinking Books and Software
Box 448
Pacific Grove, CA 93950
1-800-458-4844
FAX: 408-393-3277

Developmental Studies Center
200 Embarcadero
Suite 305
Oakland, CA 94606
1-800-666-7270
510-533-0213
FAX: 510-464-3670

Educators for Social Responsibility
23 Garden Street
Cambridge, MA 02138
1-800-370-2515
617-492-1764
FAX: 617-864-5164

Ethics Resource Center
1120 G Street NW
Suite 200
Washington, DC 20005
1-800-777-1285
202-737-2258
FAX: 202-737-2227

Giraffe Project
P. O. Box 759
Langley, WA 98260
360-221-7989
FAX: 360-221-7817

Heartwood Institute
425 N. Craig Street
Suite 302
Pittsburgh, PA 15213
1-800-432-7810
412-688-8570
FAX: 412-688-8552

Jefferson Center for Character Education
2700 East Foothill Blvd., Suite 302
Pasadena, CA 91107
818-792-8130
FAX: 818-792-8364
(Young People's Press: 619-231-9774, 1-800-231-9774)

Index

CORWIN
PRESS

The Corwin Press logo—a raven striding across an open book—represents the happy union of courage and learning. We are a professional-level publisher of books and journals for K–12 educators, and we are committed to creating and providing resources that embody these qualities. Corwin's motto is "Success for All Learners."